CW01497536

The Story of the Japanese Submarine Fleet, 1941-1945

SUNK

by **MOCHITSURA HASHIMOTO**
Former Submarine Commanding Officer, IJN

Translated by Commander **E. H. M. COLEGRAVE, RN** *(Retired)*

With an Introduction by Commander **EDWARD L. BEACH, USN**

Illustrated with Line Drawings and Photographs

SUNK

The Story of the Japanese Submarine Fleet, 1941-1945

Reprinted by Progressive Press,
PO Box 126,
Joshua Tree, Calif. USA.
May 31, 2010 ("Memorial Day")

ISBN 1-61577-581-1
EAN 978-1-61577-581-1
Printed in the USA

Library of Congress Cataloging-in-Publication Data
LCCN: 54010522 (1st ed.)
Author: Hashimoto, Mochitsura, 1909-
Main Title: Sunk; the story of the Japanese submarine fleet, 1941-1945.
Translated by E.H.M. Colegrave. With an introd. by Edward L. Beach.
First Published: New York, Henry Holt & Co. [1954]
Description: 285 p. illus. 22 cm. (Reprinted 2010)
Notes: Original title (transliterated): I-go 58 kito seri.
Subjects: World War, 1939-1945 --Naval operations, Japanese.
                World War, 1939-1945 --Naval operations --Submarine.
LC Classification: D784.J3 H3
Dewey Class No.:   940.5451

FOREWORD

What happened to Japan's submarines and what sort of fight did they put up?

As far as Japan was concerned, the recent war was waged according to a rigid strategy. There was no detailed operational planning. It was a fight in which science had been ignored. In such circumstances the submarine, always highly vulnerable unless used intelligently, was inevitably sacrificed. Throughout the war the whole submarine fleet was in reality a special attack force in which, in the absence of scientific weapons, the crews were just so much human ammunition. Today we hear much about rearmament. If money is to be spent on armaments, it should be used for scientific development. Never again must we go to war with only a bamboo lance.

The Japanese Submarine Fleet was entirely wiped out, but the martial spirits of its sailors are still with us on the far-flung oceans. In the Pacific, the Indian Ocean, and the Atlantic we remember the multitude of resentful sleeping warriors; in our ears we hear the whisper of the "voice from the bottom of the sea."

Thus, as one of the few submarine captains to survive, I have taken up my pen to try to record something of the unknown hardships and successes of our submarines.

During the past six months I have visited survivors throughout the country to collect material for my story. I wish especially to express my thanks to the U. S. Far East Naval authorities and also to the following for their kind cooperation: Mr. S. Toyoda, formerly C.-in-C. Combined Fleet; Mr. S. Fukutome, his Chief of Staff; many former naval officers, and Mr. T. Niina of the information bureau of the newspaper *Mainichi*.

MOCHITSURA HASHIMOTO

Despite the gloomy conditions under which they worked, our submarines fought well, and the grim story of Japanese submarine units has been well recorded by former Lieutenant Commander Hashimoto.

It is certainly valuable material, and I wish to recommend it as an excellent history.

S. *Toyoda*
Former C.-in-C.
Combined Fleet, IJN

For Albi.

CONTENTS

INTRODUCTION

By Commander Edward L. Beach, USN

When the fighting and the hating have died away and peace once more is established between two warring nations, then, not uncommonly, those who have but recently wielded the sword may find themselves plying the pen. To some extent there is a real need for extenuation of or justification for the part lately played in the war, and, to a lesser degree, there have been deliberate attempts to help—or influence—the writing of history. There is always a certain poignancy inherent in the frustrated aims and ambitions of the losers, and it is a natural determination on their part that praiseworthy action must not go unrecognized. It is less frequent that a military man of the losing side will write a book which cannot be interpreted otherwise than as a bitter criticism of the underlying philosophy by which his side of the war was guided.

The implication is not intended—it is in fact contradicted—that Mochitsura Hashimoto has indulged in denunciation, at least in so many words. Far from it! But the denunciation is there, buried deep between the lines of his book, and it brings with it a lesson which every military man and every student of history would do well to ponder.

Various theorists and students of the history of World War II have explained the ineffectiveness of the Japanese submarines by saying that they were improperly employed—a correct generalization, and also an extremely easy one to make. They were improperly employed, but what, exactly, was improper in their employment? What was different in their employment from ours? Were not the accepted missions of both U. S. and Japanese submarines identical at the outset of the war? Did not Japanese submarines sink the aircraft carriers *Wasp* in the South Pacific and *Yorktown* at Midway, the cruiser *Indianapolis* almost at the very end of the war, and numerous other important vessels besides?

Yet it is a matter of record that the Japanese Submarine Fleet, numbering approximately sixty vessels at the start, suffered total losses of one hundred thirty and was in effect completely wiped out without having been able to affect even slightly the course of the war.

Sunk, by my one-time enemy, Mochitsura Hashimoto, formerly Commander, Imperial Japanese Navy, and, incidentally, skipper of the submarine which torpedoed the last major war vessel of our side sunk in the war, the *Indianapolis*, tells us why. Being one of the first such public reports from any Japanese military person, it eloquently documents the basic failing of the whole Japanese effort. In so doing, it carries its own warning for us—for next time we may be the one who, anticipating the struggle, plans too thoroughly what the enemy will do.

A calm and unemotional evaluation of the Japanese Navy of 1941 ought to lead to the conclusion that ship for ship and man for man it was superior to ours. This should occasion no surprise, if the Japanese are given credit for being intelligent men and good fighters. Our navy was similarly better in detail than the British Navy in 1812. It is axiomatic that when you know whom you are going to fight you will build your ships and weapons, organize your forces, to overmatch his; whereas your adversary, deprived of that single objectivity, perhaps with a larger investment already in being, cannot, prior to the outbreak of war, rebuild or reorganize accordingly.

Under such circumstances an inherently weaker nation may temporarily achieve notable victories over the stronger. If the stronger nation is unable to meet the challenge of its enemy at the points raised, or is too in-flexible to adjust to meet the surprise threat, it might, notwithstanding its superior potential force, be beaten in a clash of arms. This was, of course, the intended evolution of the war according to the Japanese master plan. They expected to achieve their objectives—the expansion of their empire to the south—before the United States was able to recover from the initial defeats. But in this instance it was they, the aggressors, who were too inflexible with their plan of conquest; we, the defenders, turned out to possess far more of that priceless resiliency.

But this is only part of the lesson of *Sunk*. The German submarine force twice almost succeeded, single-handed, in bringing victory to Germany on the sea in the face of the everywhere prevalent superiority of Great Britain's navy. The United States submarine force brought Japan to her knees, a fact conceded by Hashimoto and by Admiral S. Fukutome, IJN, who contributes the concluding chapter to *Sunk*. Why then, specifically, the dismal failure of the Japanese Submarine Fleet?

Fukutome says it was because the Japanese Navy underestimated the U. S. submarines. For every ton of shipping she built, Japan lost three by submarine attack. Since she had to rely on the import of raw materials, steel production was severely reduced. Therefore she could build fewer ships, there was insufficient fuel for her submarines and other warships, and the vicious spiral continued.

But while we can understand how the submarine campaign would be affected, as was Japan's entire navy, by "economic strangulation," this does not explain how submarine effectiveness, particularly, came to be reduced almost to zero. The rest of the explanation lies in the inflexibility of the Japanese High Command and a strange blindness of all the Japanese military services to the realities of this war.

The tradition of the Japanese warrior since the dawn of Japanese history is that victory rides with the heroic sword, that a refusal to admit defeat insures victory, that a desperate all-out defense is bound to win. A parallel exists in our own country in the belief that true love will always triumph, and in our insistence, at least in movies and magazine fiction, upon the victory of the underdog. In Japan the difference was that the war lords believed this flapdoodle and allowed it to govern their strategy. When a part of their hastily accumulated empire was cut off, for example, orders would be issued to fight to the last man. The garrison would do so, laying down their lives in a senseless, useless, inconsequential sacrifice which, in the traditional Japanese manner, at the end became fanatical. To supply these beleaguered and bypassed outposts in an ocean now under enemy control, where all common-sense rules of warfare required withdrawal of troops while it was yet possible, some means of transportation which at least had a chance of success was required. Hence the submarines, low on the priority list for radar for self-defense and steel for replacement vessels, were pressed into service as emergency supply vessels in a succession of forlorn hopes—which is the only adequate description of their use.

Instead of being allowed to develop their own tactics in the catalyst of war, of being free to shift as the situation changed, of being commanded by submariners who, in years of service, had come to understand the problems of their trade as instinctively as a fish knows how to swim, the Japanese submarines were set to impossible, useless, and wasteful tasks by men who understood nothing about them. True to their instincts and their training, the submariners tried loyally to carry out the futile orders, and in doing so practically every ship and every man in their force, with pathetically few exceptions, were lost. Throughout Hashimoto's story he sadly chronicles the demise, one by one, of his comrades. The cumulative tale, aptly enough, is named *Sunk. The Story of the Japanese Submarine Fleet.*

At the end we have the desperate tale of the Kaitens, the human torpedoes. These were small submarines—or large torpedoes, depending on how one looked at them—fitted with a tiny compartment in which the pilot rode on his one-way mission. They were the undersea counterparts of the kamikazes, differing from Italian, British, and German human torpedoes in that no provision was made for ultimate rescue of the operator. For this reason they had greater potential utility, since they could be used in the open ocean against ships under way; and this means of increasing efficiency of course appealed to the Japanese command psychology. No attempt was made to fasten mines to the bottoms of the enemy vessels or to drop mines under their keels, as other navies did. The Japanese technique was simply to drive ahead to a collision with the target and explosion of the warhead.

These suicide subs, it should be remarked, were very different in concept, though not in ultimate employment, from the two-man boats which became notorious with the attack on Pearl Harbor. Those were real, battery-powered submarines with torpedoes which could be ejected, and the operation plans provided for their return to the parent submarines. All five launched against Pearl Harbor failed to return, however, and the attrition of these boats due to the hazards inherent in their employment made them virtually suicidal also. Then, particularly attractive to the Japanese temperament, came the idea that their range, and hence their usefulness, could be doubled if no return was to be contemplated. And so the out-and-out suicide submarine was born.

The Japanese attitude regarding the lives of their own people is shown in another way, in an anecdote in the chapter on plane-carrying submarines. A plane-carrying submarine was sent on a reconnaissance mission to Pearl Harbor. Because of the heavy defense measures there, the skipper of the submarine did not dare to stay on the surface long enough to launch his plane within the planned range of the target, or to wait around afterward to recover it. So he surfaced twice as far away and sent the ninety-mile-per-hour plane on a one-way flight, himself departing immediately and reporting the success of his stratagem with satisfaction upon his return to Japan. Hashimoto notes that the plane did arrive at Pearl Harbor and managed to radio back some information on ships there before its gasoline ran out.

It was this very readiness to expend life which made the Japanese fierce and fanatical fighters and at the same time cost them that irreplaceable resource most vital to their empire: their trained warriors—fliers, submariners, superbly conditioned professional forces. They "shot the works" in successive broadsides which totally missed the mark at Pearl Harbor, Midway, the Solomon Islands, the Gilberts, the Philippines, the Marianas, the Ryukyus—in each instance but the first one willingly accepting losses which they could ill bear and which in the end proved disastrous.

So much for the Japanese concept of war. It might have been all right for the Samurai and the Forty-seven *Ronin* who in ancient legend committed hara-kiri after avenging the death of their ruler, but it simply was not geared to 1941. And Hashimoto, though he does not plan to go quite this far, says this with excruciating clearness in his book.

One of the avowed purposes of *Sunk* is to document the failings in technical development which cost the Japanese Navy its submarine force and thereby contributed to losing the war. "Never again," says Hashimoto in his foreword, "must we go to war with only a bamboo lance." With regard to radar—a weapon, let it be stated bluntly, which had more effect on the outcome of the war than any other—one cannot but agree with him. But as a whole the facts document much, much more: the basic, pathetic, hopeless fallaciousness of the whole Japanese philosophy.

As a case specifically in point, the following conversation, which took place during the interrogations of Japanese officials after the war, is most illuminating. A passage in Rear Admiral Samuel E. Morison's *The Rising*

Sun in the Pacific, in which he characterized the Pearl Harbor attack as "idiotic" and a "strategic imbecility," was under discussion:

Japanese ex-Admiral: "Why do you call our attack on Pearl Harbor a 'strategic imbecility'?"

U. S. Lieutenant: "Without the attack there was a chance that the United States might not have declared war on Japan, or that even if we had, because of our pre-occupation with Europe and Hitler, our attempts to halt the Japanese advance to the south would not have been such an all-out effort. The one certain way to arouse America to action was to attack American soil."

Japanese ex-Admiral: "But we felt it necessary to immobilize your fleet so that we could make our move to the south free from the possibility of American offensive action."

U. S. Lieutenant: "How long, according to your calculations, was the Pearl Harbor attack to have kept the United States from making offensive moves?"

Japanese ex-Admiral: "Eighteen months was our estimate."

U. S. Lieutenant: "And how long was it before the first offensive move took place?"

Japanese ex-Admiral: "Why, fast carriers were striking the Gilberts and Marshalls at the end of January and early in February, 1942. It was less than sixty days!"

U. S. Lieutenant: "Yes. Tell me, were you aware of the location of the fuel storage tanks at Pearl Harbor?"

Japanese ex-Admiral: "Of course. Their location was well known."

U. S. Lieutenant: "And how many bombs were dropped on those tanks?"

Japanese ex-Admiral: "None. Our primary objective was your capital ships."

U. S. Lieutenant: "Had it ever occurred to your planners that if the Oahu fuel tank farm had been destroyed it would have meant that the fleet at Hawaii would have been virtually immobilized until fuel could be delivered from the mainland? And your submarines might well have interdicted such shipments and actually prevented U. S. offensives for many months?"

The answer of the Japanese admiral is not recorded, but the narrator of the episode states that his sudden pallor at the thought betrayed the novelty of this concept in his thinking. Apparently the Japanese Navy had always considered the United States fleet as their major enemy, which indeed it was, but the most logical ways and means of achieving its neutralization had never entered into their considerations. Hence the carefully planned surprise attack, an attack which actually accomplished each of its immediate objectives, had a long-range result disastrously opposite from that anticipated.

Sunk is a compilation of official and semiofficial reports, personal reminiscences of the author and others, newspaper accounts, and summations of data. This writing technique is typically Japanese and, unfortunately, is not entirely known in this country. To a large degree it also suffers from difficulties of translation. Many scholars have found it almost impossible to reproduce accurately both the spirit and thought of Japanese text. The reader must make allowances for this.

For *Sunk* is an honest book. It is written by one of our enemies, a first-class one at that, and was intended primarily for Japanese consumption. In it he tells of his and his fellows' struggle to accomplish their missions, and the heartaches they experienced when they failed, which they did most of the time. He tells of the technical problems they faced trying to get radar for their boats, their attempts to solve them, and the unreasoning opposition of the Headquarters Staff who "were more concerned with preserving their dignity than giving proper appreciation to actual service conditions." He tells of fantastically brave attempts to carry on, of desperate battles for survival under the sea—and an attrition factor, toward the end, of more than fifty per cent.

Add to all this what the U. S. submarine force learned after the war about our enemy counterpart: large boats, difficult to handle submerged, some twice as big as ours; complicated and inadequate controls; crowded living conditions and a completely foreign sanitation outlook; excessive vibration; inadequate silencing of emergency machinery; wholesale violation of safe submarining construction practices, according to our standards. The wonder was that the Japanese submariners operated at all, much less took their unhandy ships to sea and sank some of our largest men-of-war.

Sunk is no apology; Hashimoto makes no excuses and is matter of fact with his criticisms. Nor is it a masterpiece of high-flown rhetoric, but it has an innate quaintness and manner of expression all its own, through which the Japanese way of thought is at least partly captured, despite the problems of translation. It is not long on description, but occasionally much will shine between the lines; and most poignant of all, of course, are the descriptions of the Kaiten operations, wherein patriotic young men, convinced that by their sacrifice they might assist in turning the tide of war in favor of their country, go sailing off to certain, and useless, death with "Three Cheers for the Emperor!" as a pathetic final message.

A warrior cannot give more. The rest is up to his leaders.

When war broke out the United States had approximately the same number of submarines in commission as Japan. We lost fifty-two during the war, and wound up at the end with over two hundred in operation. The Japanese Navy started with sixty, lost one hundred thirty, and at the end of the conflict had something like a dozen left. "Silent Service" though we were, we lacked not for leaders who knew our needs and a country able to supply them. We fought an entirely different kind of war from that of our enemy sister service. Our problems, at the outset, were almost identical, except that the Japanese had the jump on us and had the bigger force. At the beginning skippers of both nations were feeling their way, taking no avoidable chances, spending all day submerged when within possible reach of enemy air patrols, never attacking unless fully ready in all respects, accenting always the maximum of concealment.

At that point, a few months after the outbreak of the war, the two submarine forces were about at a standoff, as far as results were concerned. As *Sunk* explains, the Japanese were greatly disappointed at the total failure of their submarine effort at Pearl Harbor. Within a few months, however, their submarines had made some heavy inroads in our combatant vessels. On our own side, the torpedo fiasco prevented effective submarine action during the first months of the war, particularly during the futile campaign to save the Philippines.

But here the paths diverge. Our submariners recognized their own shortcomings and met their difficulties head on. With enlightened leadership and practicable instructions they became more and more effective. The Japanese, on the other hand, could not adjust to meet changed or unexpected conditions. Their war plan had been made by the best military minds in the country. Ergo, the trouble they were encountering must be in the execution; it could not lie in the difficulties encountered or in the plan itself. And so the American submarine campaign, credited by experts on both sides with being the major single factor which beat Japan to her knees, waxed to overpowering strength, whereas that of our enemy waned to impotency.

This book clearly, straightforwardly, sadly of course, tries to lay the facts on the line for us.

Historically, the reader will have great interest in checking such facts as he might have known or experienced against accounts of the same actions as given by Hashimoto. For myself, there is the matter of the U. S. submarine *Grunion*, sunk—so far as we can tell—on July 30, 1942, off Kiska in the Aleutians. There is a discrepancy in the facts as we know them and as Hashimoto has them. Hashimoto says that a colleague of his, Meiji Tagami, skipper of the Japanese submarine I-25, sank a United States submarine during the return voyage from his third trip to the Oregon coast, some time in October. It is evident that Tagami errs in his timing, and he should have said that he sank the American submarine while returning from his second mission to America, late in July. There was no other American submarine lost in the Aleutians, with the single exception of S-27, which ran aground and from which the personnel were rescued. The submarine Tagami sank must have been the *Grunion*.

The *Trigger* was also in the Aleutians at that time and I, as Communications Officer, happened to be in the radio room when we intercepted the last message *Grunion* ever transmitted. Our radio operator and I both noted the change from the measured pace of the early message groups to the hurried jumble of the last few, and it has since become my conviction that *Grunion* actually was under attack or might even have been mortally wounded at that very moment. The collision alarm must have been sounded as soon as Tagami's torpedo was sighted; perhaps even the fatal explosion might have already taken place. It was natural for the radio operator, nearly finished with transmitting a message, to attempt to bang out hurriedly the last few groups during the half-minute or so before his radio antenna went under.

For the next twenty-four hours after *Grunion's* message was sent, our headquarters in Dutch Harbor tried to raise her in order to get a repeat on the last few message groups, but she never answered again.

Her last message related to recent action with Japanese antisubmarine craft in the course of which *Grunion* believed she had sunk two and damaged several others, and had expended all of her torpedoes in the after torpedo room. Until reading Tagami's account, first partially published in a newspaper and now more fully explained in *Sunk,* I had been of the opinion that one of the antisubmarine craft must have trapped the unfortunate American submarine.

Another account of consuming interest to Americans must be the Japanese submarine view of the attack on Pearl Harbor. For them it was a somewhat frustrating experience. So far as they knew, no success whatever had been achieved, either by the midget submarines or by the large I-class ocean cruisers sent to Hawaii. Hashimoto was along on that operation as Torpedo Officer of the I-24, and describes the operation from that point of view. The midget submarines were launched after great difficulty, illustrative of the ability of the sea to ferret out weaknesses and foil the best-laid plans. Of the five midget submarines launched, none returned to their parent submarines. None apparently expected to return; it was in fact Japan's first suicide mission of World War II.

The big submarines remained outside the harbor for several days in their unsuccessful attempt to rendezvous with the midgets. No United States vessels were sighted except destroyers, and as a result of air and surface activity there was no opportunity for submarine attack on the United States fleet. The whole operation from their point of view was a failure.

It is surprising that the Japanese should have had this reaction, or that the failure of submarines to make a decisive contribution to the Pearl Harbor attack should have been of any importance, but to the Oriental mind it was. "Face" to the Japanese means much more than its literal translation in this country. In America, if one loses face, it is usually a transient thing of only passing embarrassment. In Japan the stigma is more severe, and more enduring.

Japanese submarines lost face at Pearl Harbor. Although the operation was planned as a double-pronged attack from submarines and aircraft, all damage was done by the carrier-borne planes.

Japanese submarines seem never to have recovered from this initial loss of face. The midget crews were made much of, given a posthumous double promotion, and their memory lionized throughout Japan. But nothing much could be done to salvage face for the big submarines. And this resulted in a lowering of their position on the priority list for essential equipment, material, and funds. It also resulted in their demands for radar being shunted aside, and ultimately in their being relegated to the role of supplying by-passed garrisons with the desperate essentials for subsistence.

The non-Oriental will feel that perhaps too much is made of these consequences of the Pearl Harbor action. But, witness another incident not related in *Sunk:* Some ten thousand balloons were released in Japan in an attempt to transport incendiaries and light bombs via high-level ocean winds to America. About nine hundred of these landed, causing forest fires and some personnel casualties in the states of Washington, Oregon, and California. Not one word of these successes was ever published or permitted in any way to get back to Japan.

Major General Kusaba, the officer in charge of this operation, which had been conceived in retaliation for the Doolittle raid, was forced to terminate his activity just as he was on the verge of introducing a larger and improved balloon missile. His explanation, when interrogated after the war, was that he had been unable to show any results of the balloon campaign and that, having lost face, he was summarily removed and the whole operation canceled. Even after the surrender he is recorded as still being "brokenhearted" at the outcome.

Among other things, this particular anecdote is an illustration of the importance of not confirming to the enemy what in normal circumstances one might expect he already knows.

The sinking of USS *Indianapolis* on July 31, 1945, described from the Japanese point of view by the skipper of the submarine involved (Hashimoto's own I-58), will be of great interest to the American reader. Knowing of the predilection of the Japanese for use of Kaitens and from what I had been able to glean regarding circumstances of the attack, it had heretofore been my belief that one or more human torpedoes must have been used against the *Indianapolis*. Despite the fact that Hashimoto did carry Kaitens on that last cruise, however, he states that he had no need to use them on this particular target. Although the Kaiten crews kept requesting permission to make the attack, Hashimoto says he refused because of the low visibility of the night and the resulting possibility that the Kaitens would be unable to press home an attack. He writes, "I determined not to use them unless the ordinary torpedo attack failed."

Little is related regarding the tactics of the approach. The *Indianapolis* was not zigzagging. I-58 came in sixty degrees on her starboard bow and commenced firing at a range of less than fifteen hundred yards. Six torpedoes were fired in a spread, and three hits were obtained. Hashimoto saw the hits through his periscope and heard additional explosions within the hull of the stricken cruiser. The Kaitens again asked to be sent to finish her off, but, according to Hashimoto, "Once launched they were gone for good, and it seemed a pity to risk wasting them." He went deep to reload his torpedoes, came back to periscope depth approximately one hour later, and, seeing nothing anywhere about, made off to the northeast with moral certainty that his target, which he had believed was an *Idaho*-class battleship, had been sunk.

There are, nevertheless, strange factors in Hashimoto's description of the attack. At fifteen hundred yards or less, which he describes as the firing range, Japanese torpedoes should have struck the side of the *Indianapolis* within one minute after firing. According to Hashimoto there was time, after firing, to bring I-58 to a course parallel with the target. The maneuver would have taken a U. S. submarine approximately three minutes. He also says, "Every minute seemed an age." I, too, have used such phraseology to describe the wait for torpedo explosions, but if the word "minute" is to be taken literally, we have a second indication that the torpedo run was actually several minutes in length.

For U. S. submarines, fifteen hundred yards range, sixty degrees on the target's bow, is an ideal firing position. U. S. or Japanese torpedoes would strike home so quickly—within about forty seconds—that there would be no time to swing to a course parallel with the enemy, nor any inclination to do so. Were a torpedo run of several minutes to be accepted, then Kaitens are positively indicated. Despite Hashimoto's unequivocal assertion to the contrary, only Kaitens could fulfill the conditions of attack as he gave them. All doubts in my mind, therefore, are far from resolved. Maybe he did use Kaitens, but, if so, why deny the fact in 1954?

The day after the atomic bomb was dropped on Nagasaki, Hashimoto, according to his account, attacked a United States convoy, releasing two Kaitens against it. He states that two destroyers were sunk. On August 12 he released a third Kaiten and sank what he describes as a fifteen-thousand-ton seaplane carrier. Records on our side do not indicate the loss of two destroyers on August 10 or anything resembling a "seaplane carrier" on August 12 by submarine torpedo or by any other means. But we do know that *Indianapolis* received three torpedo hits. The thought automatically intrudes that perhaps Hashimoto had to make up the later attacks in order to account for his last three Kaitens!

The last part of Hashimoto's narrative describes the receipt of the news that the war had ended and that Japan had accepted the inevitability of surrender. The Japanese language, especially as translated into English, is unable to depict the emotion with which the news must have been received. Hashimoto says, "The seaman wireless rating had tears in his eyes." One must try to put one's self in his position to attempt an appreciation of what must have been, to them, the ultimate catastrophe.

On August 18, 1945, I-58 returned to Kure, and, despite a few hotheads whom the author characterizes as "all for going out to fight," she and her remaining sisters complied with the Imperial decree of surrender.

Persons who have spent years in Japan since the war and have gained a deep understanding of that country have commented that this single defeat will not keep the Japanese warlike spirit down forever. At the moment, true, there is opposition to rearmament even for their own protection, but there are others in Japan, like Hashimoto, who revere the valiant deeds of their warriors, their kamikazes, and their Kaitens. The latter are fortunate, as Hashimoto put it, that they did not survive to suffer the indignity of defeat; their spirits bear witness to the sufferings they underwent and the cause they gave their all, unavailingly, to save. Says Hashimoto, "In the Pacific, the Indian Ocean, and the Atlantic we remember the multitude of resentful sleeping warriors; in our ears we hear the whisper of the 'voice from the bottom of the sea.' "

Japan is a continuing challenge to America, a challenge more subtle, perhaps more difficult to resolve, than the one she posed in 1941. The Japanese are an energetic people, fundamentally a fine people. The challenge is whether or not we shall be able to convince them permanently of the good things inherent in our way of life. The strength of Japan, if it can be channeled toward permanent espousal of the cause of freedom, can make her our strongest ally in the Far Eastern world.

1

SPECIAL

OPERATION

AT PEARL

HARBOR

In November, 1941, I was the torpedo officer of submarine I-24. She had left the builder's yard only six months previously, and I had been very busy fitting her out since the summer. On our maiden voyage from Sasebo to Kure, the trials we carried out en route were barely satisfactory, but on arrival at Kure on November 10 we were attached immediately to the third flotilla of the 1st Submarine Squadron, under the command of Captain Sasaki. Shortly afterward orders were received to prepare for active service.

The responsibility for these preparations devolved on me. Though the I-class submarines were large, there was insufficient space to carry three months' provisions, and all the gangways and every available corner were stowed to capacity. Final trials occupied a week of hectic activity. We sailed from Kure harbor equipped with some odd-looking hangarlike gear, to be used for launching midget submarines, and carried out trials at sea under the supervision of dockyard officials. On return to harbor a defect in the main tank had to be remedied which took the whole night. We realized that war was imminent and waited with mingled eagerness and dread to learn what part we should have to play. At a gathering of submarine officers at the Naval Club on November 17, the night before we left on our first mission, conditions at Hawaii were the chief subject of conversation; this was the first time we had any inkling of our destination. We were informed that Pearl Harbor, the base of the U. S. Pacific Fleet, was to be attacked by midget submarines.

The idea of midget submarines originated in 1936, when a submarine officer attached to the Naval Staff saw a small one-man underwater craft being used for fishing operations.

A parent ship was specially constructed to carry out experiments. In the early part of 1941 intensive trials were carried out, and in October, 1941, the sponsors of the midget submarine proposed plans for a submarine attack on Pearl Harbor should hostilities break out. The proposal was agreed to, provided that a plan of recovery could be included and provided that no attempt was to be made to enter the bay. Planning went ahead on these lines and five submarines were equipped to carry midgets. When the plan was complete it was put up to the Commander-in-Chief Combined Fleet by the Admiral Commanding Submarines. However, the plan submitted provided for the entry of the midgets inside the bay and the C.-in-C., Admiral Yamamoto, declared, "If they go inside the bay they can never return, and such entry is unnecessary." The matter was put to the prospective midget crews themselves, and as they were one and all firmly decided in their minds that entry into the bay was possible, the authorities eventually gave way and the plan was allowed to stand. The C.-in-C., however, insisted that detailed plans be made for recovery, and so when we received our final orders for the attack, we were instructed to stand by to pick up crews, should any survive.

It seemed an audacious plan, and, considering our lack of training in this type of attack and indeed our inexperience in actual warfare, we could not help feeling somewhat anxious, though I myself had seen action on the Yangtse when serving in gunboats and mine sweepers.

We were to leave Kure the following day, November 18: five submarines carrying midget submarines on a mission involving almost certain death.

With our load of midget submarines we set forth on our journey, heading for the Pacific via the Inland Sea and the Bungo Channel. It was a moonless night. As we left harbor, lights resembling a merchant ship were sighted on a parallel course. They accompanied us for some time before we eventually outdistanced them; we proceeded submerged, for we did not want to give away the fact that we were carrying the midgets. At dawn inspection through the periscope showed that the ship we had taken for a merchantman was in fact an aircraft carrier. We therefore surfaced and proceeded in company.

Off Tosa we adopted three-watch submerged cruising stations. The crew started intensive training. The senior officer of the squadron asked if we were feeling confident, and I heard the captain reply that he would do his best, that and nothing more.

At that time, the only submarines equipped to carry midgets were the five I-16-class boats which comprised the 1st Submarine Squadron, and they were to play a vital part in the forthcoming attack. They were of recent construction, and the crews were fresh and untrained, so it was a question of sending them out and hoping for the best. Diving-stations drill was carried out three times a day until the crews were proficient in crash-diving. Our orders included a warning to be on the lookout for enemy detection devices, but we knew little of what to expect in that direction.

At length we altered course to the eastward and made for Hawaii. The five submarines were spread out at intervals of twenty miles. The first and second submarine units, comprising eleven ships, had already left Yoko-suka and were advancing on a great circular course to the northward so as to pass between the Aleutian Islands and Midway Island. The third submarine unit, comprising nine ships, was pressing on to Hawaii from the advance base at Kwajalein, passing midway between Johnston and Howland islands. Our unit was taking the direct route to Hawaii between Johnston and Howland islands. This involved a security risk, for there was a chance of discovery by enemy patrols, but since the fitting out of the unit had been delayed and it was consequently late in sailing, there was no alternative.

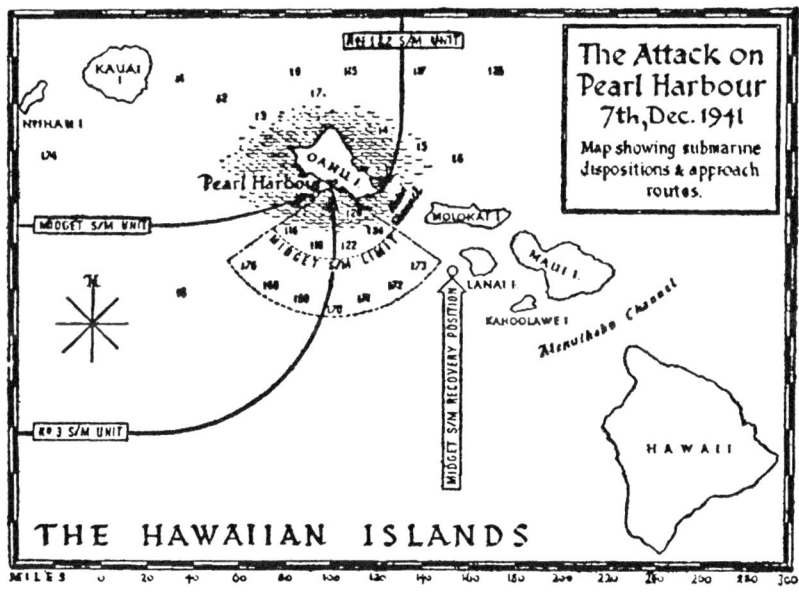

The Attack on
Pearl Harbour
7th, Dec. 1941

Map showing submarine
dispositions & approach
routes.

THE HAWAIIAN ISLANDS

As we proceeded on the surface, all was quiet. There was nothing to see except clouds and the endless expanse of sea. By day, work on the midgets was carried out on the upper deck. Down below, officers were working out the attack plans on the charts of Hawaii. When we entered Wake Island air patrol area we were submerged by day and only proceeded on the surface by night. These long periods submerged were excellent from a training point of view, but the air inside the boat grew foul and the temperature rose, making one feel sleepy.

On November 26 we received a report to the effect that negotiations with the U.S.A. were now hopeless. At the same time, we learned that there were two battleships and several other craft at anchor in Pearl Harbor. I remember thinking that the number of battleships was disappointing. On December 2, we heard that hostilities were to begin on the 7th. On the eve of that day eight battleships and several other ships were reported in Pearl Harbor. The fact that there were no aircraft carriers was a little disappointing, but at that time battleships were the most important capital ships, and we were inwardly very pleased.

As the time for action grew near, final torpedo tests had to be carried out. This involved drawing the torpedoes out of their tubes while the submarine was submerged. It was dangerous for the boat to be at an angle while the torpedoes were being worked upon. As usual, I was standing alongside the officer of the watch in the control room to see that everything was in order, when suddenly the boat grew heavy and started to sink. The navigator who was on watch instantly ordered, "Blow the forward trimming tanks," but this and running the pumps failed to have any effect, and the boat continued to sink. We tried a burst of speed but it was too late. I dashed to the torpedo compartment, where I found that the forward trimming tank blow valve was jammed. Nothing would move it. The boat went on sinking and confusion reigned. The depth-gauge needle began to move faster. Soon the boat would be crushed by the pressure of water. I attacked the jammed valve wheel again with a wheel spanner. At last it gave, opening the valve and admitting air into the tanks. At first we went on sinking, but soon the downward movement stopped, the depth gauge came back from the three-hundred-foot mark; we had started to come up. The discharge pump began to work and the lightened submarine speedily shot to the surface. Before submerging again the trim was adjusted accurately. The normal maximum safe diving depth for these submarines was three hundred feet, with a certain margin of safety up to some four hundred and fifty feet: it would have been fatal had we gone on sinking. It was unpleasant to think how near we had come to disappearing in the depths of the Pacific before we had even begun to fight.

That night when we surfaced, intending to work as usual on the midget, we had a shock. Owing to the great depth to which we had sunk, a torpedo was crushed and jammed in its tube. We had to work all night getting a spare one up from below. This operation may sound easy enough but in fact it was far from simple. The lack of space on the narrow upper deck made transporting something weighing over a ton to the after-end of the boat no mean task, to say nothing of having to dispose of the damaged torpedo quietly over the side.

As we drew near to Hawaii the sea became rougher.

Every night preparation of the midget submarine continued: charging the batteries, topping-up with air, and lining up the torpedo tubes had to be carried out in difficult conditions because the upper deck of the submarine was usually awash. We were due off Pearl Harbor on the night of December 6. At last Hawaii came in sight, proving the skill of our navigating officer.

In accordance with our instructions, we arrived at a position eight miles from Pearl Habor. Reports showed that the other submarines were also in position. As we lay concealed, we could see the bright lights on shore and the neon signs on Waikiki beach. There were some dazzling lights which we took to be searchlights. The rows of lamps on the aerodrome were clearly visible and we could hear a radio churning out jazz music. It was close on 11 P.M. and the enemy was completely unaware of our presence. At the last moment one of the crew carrying out final tests on the midget submarine reported a gyro failure. The time for launching was approaching rapidly. There seemed no prospect of correcting the fault in time. By then all other preparations had been completed and the crew embarked. The gunnery officer of I-24 had visited Hawaii during his training cruise when a midshipman and he was pointing out various details connected with the entrance to Pearl Harbor to the captain of the midget crew. Eleven o'clock, the appointed hour for the launching, passed, and still the gyro resisted all efforts to put it right. At 1 A.M. it was decided to go ahead without the gyro. The officer commanding the midget went calmly up to the bridge to make his final report and then took his place in the midget. The parent submarine dived, the securing clamps were cast off, and the midget was off to the Pearl Harbor entrance.

At 7:55 A.M. the air attack on Pearl Harbor started. The sea was rough and the waves high. Even at a depth of ninety feet, we were rolling five degrees. Just after 8:25 A.M., faint sounds could be heard from the direction of Pearl Harbor, but no ships could be seen. The submarine tended to rise and sink due to the swell. We made every effort to keep her down. She would get heavier and start to sink till we couldn't see through the periscope, and then when we ran the pump on the trimming tanks she rose again and tended to break surface. The pumps were going almost continuously. At length, in full daylight, the boat broke surface. This was no time to be caught in full view. We quickly flooded all the trimming tanks, putting in about twenty tons of water, but she refused to sink. From the captain came the order, "Hurry—two float reconnaissance planes in sight." Eventually we managed to get down to ninety feet but even there we were rolling five degrees either side. Then we found a defect in the main ballast pump used for trimming and we were unable to prevent the boat from becoming slightly bow-heavy. We hoped fervently that we wouldn't be caught in this state by the enemy. We were exceedingly uncomfortable. I kept looking at my watch, longing for sunset, when it would be safe for us to surface.

After our return to Japan, we heard that an American broadcast in "Clear" had been intercepted, reporting an enemy submarine ten miles south of Barber's Point: this was most probably I-24. At the time, however, the enemy was fully occupied with the air attack and seemed to have had no time to hunt submarines outside the bay. On that first day of the war, we saw no enemy ships nor were we attacked by gunfire or depth charges. After dark, following routine procedure, high-pressure air was admitted to the main ballast tanks. Instead of surfacing on an even keel the boat heeled over alarmingly to starboard. Quickly the air to the port tank was shut off, but still she heeled over. Hasty inspection proved that a main vent was not properly closed, being jammed open by a piece of wood which fortunately was easily removed. It was just a month since the ship had been completed and bits of rubbish remaining over from the building yard had been the cause of many minor defects. Everything had been thoroughly cleaned before sailing, but something lodged in a pipe had worked out and caused us this trouble on the enemy's doorstep. Once the vent was cleared we were able to surface and proceed at full speed to the midget submarine recovery area. In a calm sea we approached to a position where it was just possible to discern the gray outline of the island. Our consorts, too, were in sight. Reports of the results of the air attack kept coming in but there was no news at all of the midget submarines. The five parent submarines lay waiting but there was no sign of the smaller fry.

On the day after the attack, while submerged, we heard what sounded like depth charges at the entrance to the bay. We thought this was probably an attack on the submarines of the 3rd Squadron who were stationed there. We waited a whole day beyond the appointed time, but there was still no sign of the midgets, and instructions were received to abandon any idea of recovery and return to Kwajalein.

The officers commanding these craft seemed to have set out with the idea that they would not return. After the launching, their private possessions, left in the parent submarine, had been set in order. They had duly left messages of farewell to their parents and directions for forwarding certain private effects. Their money was all left with their servants. These preparations were justified, for not one returned.

The midget launched from my submarine had been delayed by gyro failure. It arrived, after many vicissitudes, at the entrance to the bay but was sighted by an enemy destroyer and depth-charged. It made a further attempt to enter the bay but the gyro continued to play tricks and it twice ran aground. Then it tried to make for the recovery position but finally ran aground and failed to get off. It was impossible to fire the torpedo, and the crew, overcome by foul gas, were captured and made prisoner.

As torpedo officer I was responsible for the midget submarine, but my duty was limited to launching. I saw such craft for the first time at Kure and had no opportunity to learn anything of their construction. There had been very little time for us to get to know the craft, and the decision to use them seems to have been very sudden. Only one of the midgets penetrated right into the bay, where it attacked the battleship *Arizona*. Two of them were reported missing and the fourth was sunk outside the bay.* The entrance to the bay had been closed by antisubmarine nets. The nets were opened just before 8 A.M., allowing one midget to slip through. Thus the results achieved by our submarines were very poor when compared with the devastation wrought by the carrier-borne aircraft.

We got back to Kwajalein at the end of December and celebrated the New Year there. Everyone was in very good spirits on account of the Pearl Harbor success. A vast crowd of natives put on a dancing display and a carefree day was spent by all.

---

* The mine sweeper USS *Condor*, on routine sweeping patrol at Pearl Harbor entrance, reported sighting a periscope, and a Catalina aircraft also sighted a midget submarine trailing USS *Antares*, perhaps hoping to slip into harbor in her wake. The destroyer *Ward* sank this midget submarine with gunfire and depth charges. The midget that crept through the open antitorpedo nets was sunk in the harbor by the destroyer *Monaghan*.

2

THE

EASTERN

PACIFIC

The early months of the war were full of incidents—unpleasant, exciting, tedious.

In December, submarine I-169 had an alarming adventure. While keeping watch at the Pearl Harbor entrance she ran foul of what appeared to be antisubmarine nets, and was so firmly held that nothing would move her. She went ahead, went astern, lightened the tanks, let water into the tanks, all without result. During these operations enemy destroyers were thrashing around overhead, so there was constant danger of being picked up by their hydrophones. As it was impossible to operate the ventilator for regulating the air supply, the carbon dioxide increased in the boat until breathing was painful. These conditions gradually got worse; the whole crew was in danger of suffocation. Desperately, they tried once more going full speed astern, and suddenly the boat freed itself from the net. By this time the air was very bad so there was nothing for it but to surface and fight it out with the destroyers. The officers and crew had a "last meal" consisting of all their favorite things and, bracing themselves for the worst, came to the surface—to an anticlimax! There were no destroyers in sight and only the eerie darkness remained. There was still the possibility that the enemy might show up, and in fact the destroyers did reappear suddenly and I-169 made a crash dive. The dive was long and deep, but the ten minutes on the surface had been long enough to expel the bad air; and in any event the destroyers soon made off—they hadn't spotted the submarine. At that time they were not equipped with radar, and the submarine owed her escape to the efficiency of her lookout technique.

Submarine I-170 failed to return from the Pearl Harbor operation and we heard after the war that she had been bombed by a Dauntless dive bomber from the carrier *Enterprise*. Badly damaged, she was unable to dive and was later finished off and sunk by another aircraft.*

I-24 left harbor again on January 3, 1942, for another patrol off Hawaii. On January 10, we received a report from another submarine that she had sighted a *Lexington*-class aircraft carrier. We joined up with the 2nd Submarine Squadron and set off in pursuit. Having obtained the carrier's course by D/F bearings, we continued the pursuit for two days at a surface speed of twenty knots. Unfortunately we again developed a defect in the buoyancy-tank valve which had been repaired at Kwajalein on our return from our first patrol. However, we made temporary repairs and were able to crash-dive when necessary.

On the afternoon of January 12, submarine I-6 suddenly sighted an enemy carrier. She dived and attacked, making hits with two torpedoes. At the time we thought that the enemy carrier had been sunk. Actually, though damaged, she was able to get away. However, this partial success considerably raised the morale of all the submarines taking part in the operation.

One Saturday about a week later, while lying in wait for targets in the enemy's traffic base off the northeast coast of Hawaii and proceeding submerged at a depth of ninety feet, we suddenly heard the sound of successive explosions. We surmised that an aircraft was dropping bombs and we wondered how we had been sighted.

* I-170 was sunk about two hundred miles northeast of Oahu.

After a pause, the captain raised the periscope, but there were no oil patches to be seen. The reason for the attack remained obscure. Perhaps the search aircraft was merely jettisoning its bombs in the sea, on completing its routine flight.

Targets were scarce and on January 20 we decided to return to home waters, after bombarding Midway Island en route as instructed. On the evening of January 22 we silently approached the island in company with submarine I-18. It was a starlit night and the lookouts were all keyed up, for the island was very near. When a little closer, we sighted what seemed to be a patrol craft and dived to avoid being spotted. Shortly afterward we surfaced and managed to identify Midway Island before darkness set in. At dawn we dived again. During the approach we had sighted a large merchant ship at anchor. Torpedo tubes were brought to the ready but alas, it transpired that the ship was on the other side of a reef. Thus all we could do was to wait for the appointed time for the bombardment. There was a lot of argument during the midday meal as to whether we should still open fire if we were not on time at the appointed position. I was all for getting on with it and when we surfaced to start the bombardment our submarine had still five minutes on hand. As first lieutenant I was in charge of the trimming operations down below and knew nothing of what was going on outside. After we had fired two or three rounds, there was some return fire from the shore batteries. The buoyancy tanks were being filled in preparation for a crash dive but the order came sooner than

I expected. However, we got her down without mishap. According to the captain we had attacked what looked like an aircraft hangar and a fire started up at the fifth round. It was in fact the flashes from the guns ashore and not a hit as we had hoped. The first salvos from the shore fell quite near the bow of the submarine and they undoubtedly came from the shore forts. We had intended to fire seven rounds but had to dive with one round still on deck. Submarine I-18 was fired on by the enemy without getting off a single round, and the bombardment was thus a complete failure. It would have been better to have waited for the ship at anchor to leave harbor.

After proceeding submerged for about four hours, we surfaced and turned westward in the teeth of a rising sea. We ran into very heavy weather off the Bonins and the boat was taking it in green against the glass screens of the bridge. I had turned over my watch to the navigating officer and had gone below to take off my wet things. Suddenly broken glass came tumbling down through the hatch and a voice was heard calling for help. I hurried up to the bridge and found everyone up there, including the captain, covered with blood. The force of the waves had broken the glass bridge-screens and everyone was cut and bleeding. I had to take over the watch again and render first aid.

3

SUBMARINE

SUCCESSES

While operations were being carried out at Pearl Harbor and off the North American coast, landings were being effected in the Philippines and Malaya. In these two areas old submarines were being used. The ten vessels of the 4th Submarine Squadron, commanded by Rear Admiral Y. Yoshitomi operating off the Malay

Peninsula, were dispersed to cover any sorties by the British fleet at Singapore in the direction of the landings and to cut off their lines of communication in the rear. The landings carried out on the east coast of the Malay Peninsula at dawn on December 7 were mostly successful except at Kota Bharu. On this day our reconnaissance planes had reported two British battleships at anchor in Singapore. At 3:15 P.M. the next day two battleships were sighted by I-165 at a point three hundred miles north of Singapore. She recognized them as the *Prince of Wales* and *Repulse*. The ships were proceeding northward at high speed; their target was the supply line of our landings. Although they were clearly visible, they were out of torpedo range, but Commander Harada, I-165's captain, sent off a cipher message giving course and bearings. It duly reached the Malayan operational H.Q., and all submarines in the area surfaced and immediately took up the pursuit at speed.* The entire Malayan naval force, consisting of the battleships *Kongo* and *Haruna*, together with the cruiser squadron and destroyer squadron under the command of Vice-Admiral Nobutake Kondo, was not really a match for the opponents, but our ships forged ahead with all speed in the hope of forcing a night action, in which was their best chance of achieving good results. However, contact

---

* HMS *Prince of Wales* and *Repulse* were sighted by a Japanese submarine at 2 P.M., December 9, 1941, in position 7° N. latitude, 105° E. longitude, steering north. (This position was very inaccurate.)

At 3:15 A.M., December 10, the Japanese received a report from a second submarine which indicated that the British squadron was steering south. Bad weather precluded any form of air search on December 9.

From a British source, Japanese submarines were reported off Singapore on December 3, 1941.

with the enemy was lost in the dark night. At 3:40 A.M. on December 10, I-156 attacked the ships on a southerly course in a position slightly to the west of the original sighting, but missed in the darkness. At dawn the air units, keyed up with the news from Pearl Harbor, joined in their search for the enemy, and by their bombs the two battleships were dispatched to the bottom of the sea. This was the first time battleships had ever been sunk by aircraft—a severe shock to the British Navy. From that day battleships yielded their place to aircraft carriers as "capital ships."

While pride of place in this operation must be given to our aircraft, it was the submarines which sent in the first report and confirmed the position of the two ships, and success was the result of submarine and aircraft cooperation.

In building up his operational plan, the C.-in-C. Combined Fleet had to decide priorities: the first consideration in planning was to ascertain accurately the scale of enemy activity. It was particularly important to find out what units were likely to be opposed to our main fleets. There were various methods of acquiring this information, of which observation by aircraft was the most reliable and readily accessible method. Since the radius of action of reconnaissance aircraft was low, great results were expected of submarine-borne aircraft.

The size of our submarines had been gradually increasing, resulting in an increase in the effective range of the aircraft, and the Japanese Navy had made great efforts before the war to develop this type of submarine. Preliminary trials carried out with aircraft borne by submarine I-5 led to the adoption of new submarine designs which made it possible to mount a catapult. At the outbreak of war eleven submarines had been equipped to carry aircraft. These included I-7, 8, 10, 15, 17, 19, 21, 23, and 26. Subsequently further types of submarine-borne aircraft were built, and by the end of the war a total of twenty-four aircraft-carrying submarines had been built: i.e., nineteen boats numbered I-27 to I-45, and I-54, 56, 58, 11, and 12.

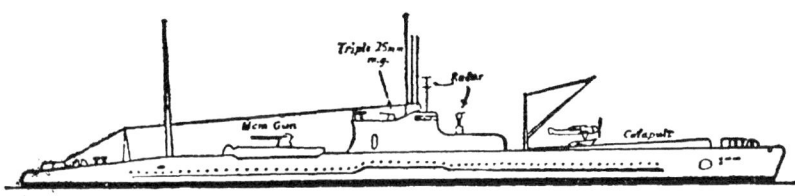

I-15-class submarine, equipped to carry a reconnaissance aircraft. See Appendix A.

The aircraft carried were all small, one-man seaplanes with a speed of only ninety knots and a period of operation of about three hours. Being very small and carrying nothing beyond a W/T set, they were no match for fighters, and if spotted by an enemy plane it was the end.

Since it took an hour to get the plane housed on board, there were times when the submarine had to abandon the aircraft and dive. In view of the weakness of these aircraft, it was the usual plan to launch them just before dawn and re-embark them by sunrise; if the weather was rough, it was often very difficult for these machines to make a landing, so that this type of reconnaissance was accompanied by many dangers. However, owing to the efforts of experienced commanding officers and the calmness of the personnel in general, many valuable reports were sent to the High Command with little loss of time.

Among the pilots flying from submarines, Warrant Officer Fujita was outstanding. He achieved four thousand flying hours and his calmness and courage greatly facilitated launching and embarking operations.

As it would be almost impossible to sight such a small object as a submarine on the return flight, arrangements were always made for a fixed rendezvous which had to be made with absolute accuracy. The usual practice was to launch the aircraft near the enemy territory concerned; then the submarine would wait about for the aircraft to return, keeping in constant W/T communication. To the submarine waiting for sunrise, with the constant thought of being taken unawares by an enemy reconnaissance, this was an unpleasant experience. The plane could be expected to return in, say, half an hour, but after alighting, about an hour was needed to prepare the boat to dive, making a total time of two and a half hours on the surface.

Sometimes during preparations for launching, the wings of the aircraft were damaged. While repairs were being carried out, the pilot would fume with impatience. For practice launches, the engines of the aircraft would be started ten to fifteen minutes after surfacing, but in the vicinity of the enemy, a period of thirty minutes to an hour was normally allowed, to insure that the submarine was not detected.

Simultaneously with the outbreak of war, I-10 and 26 were ordered to carry out a reconnaissance of Fiji, Samoa, and Tutuila and the Aleutian archipelago respectively, to be completed by December 5, 1941. These boats left Yokosuka on November 16 and 19 respectively, and both achieved their object without resorting to the use of aircraft. I-10 sighted the American cruiser *Astoria* off Pagopago in the Fiji Islands on December 4, but nothing else worthy of note.

On December 17, 1941, I-5's aircraft carried out a dawn reconnaissance of Pearl Harbor and provided a good report on the damage inflicted by our task forces at the outbreak of war. In January, 1942, I-9's aircraft made a further reconnaissance of Pearl Harbor on her return to Kwajalein from the North American coast.

I-25 left Kwajalein on February 8, 1942, and in two months achieved successful reconnaissance results on the east coast of Australia and the principal harbors of New Zealand, returning to Japan early in April. Her aircraft had flown over Sydney, Melbourne, Hobart, Wellington, Auckland, and Suva and she also had reported on Pagopago.

In the Indian Ocean I-17 was instructed to make an air reconnaissance of Colombo and Trincomalee but, owing to the strict enemy patrols, failed to carry out the order.

In May, 1942, at the time of the Midway and Aleutian operations, submarines I-25 and 26 left Yokosuka to carry out an air reconnaissance of Kodiak in the Aleutian archipelago. As I-25 was trying to launch her aircraft in the vicinity of Dutch Harbor, in the dawn light of the long northern summer, she sighted an enemy cruiser. The captain was in a dilemma but decided to send off the machine according to plan. The cruiser passed by. Later an enemy destroyer appeared on the scene, though by good fortune the aircraft had been recovered and the boat was able to dive to safety. At the same time I-19, surprised by an enemy aircraft when preparing to launch her own aircraft, had to dive and abandon her machine.

Submarine-borne air reconnaissance was continued till 1944, gradually becoming more hazardous owing to increasing enemy patrol activities. On August 19, 1943, I-17 was attacked and sunk by enemy aircraft while carrying out a reconnaissance off Noumea, to the southeast of the Solomon Islands.

In August, 1942, an attack was carried out on the American mainland in retaliation for the air raid on Tokyo by an enemy task force of B-25 aircraft. Our plan was to make an attack with incendiary bombs on the forest belt. The planes used were a small type, submarine-borne, specially fitted to carry two seventy-six-kilogram incendiary bombs each. Submarine I-25, commanded by Commander Meiji Tagami, carrying six of these special bombs, left Yokosuka for the attack on August 15, 1942. Taking a great circular route, I-25 arrived off the coast of Oregon after about a fortnight's voyage, but owing to bad weather in which it was impossible to launch or recover the aircraft, the boat cruised to the south of Cape Blanco to wait for the weather to improve.

At about an hour before sunrise on a day in mid-September, in a position about six miles south of Cape Blanco lighthouse, the aircraft was launched. The pilot was Warrant Officer Fujita. Two bombs were dropped on the forest belt about fifty miles southeast of Cape Blanco and, having observed white smoke rising from the target, the plane returned to the submarine which had been waiting on the surface for two hours. These incendiary bombs were of a specially powerful type which generated a temperature of about one thousand five hundred degrees within a radius of three hundred yards, and the objective was therefore effectively attained. It is thought that considerable fires were started, as the American radio stations broadcasted that several people were killed.

The second attack was made from a position about ten miles to the west of Cape Blanco, two hours after sunset on a moonlit night. When Fujita returned to the rendezvous, fifty miles east of the cape, he had difficulty in locating the submarine, but fortunately some oil floating on the surface made a track which enabled him to find his way.

By the end of September there was much fog, and as the weather became worse in October, launching and dispatch of aircraft became impossible, and operations had to be discontinued.

During the early half of October, I-25 sank two oilers off the west coast of America and with her remaining torpedo attacked and sank a U. S. submarine. I-25 returned to home waters at the end of the month.

Meanwhile, submarines had found another duty. In March, 1942, a heavy attack on Pearl Harbor was planned, using flying boats. Submarine I-22, detailed to prepare a fueling base en route, made use of the atoll French Frigate Shoal.* She also carried out a preliminary reconnaissance between Hawaii and Midway Island. At the end of February, submarines I-15, 19, and 26 took on supplies of aviation fuel and proceeded to the atoll in preparation for the operation. I-9 took up a position between Jaluit in the Marshall Islands and French Frigate Shoal as a radio homing unit.

Large Type-2 flying boats, which had the largest range of action, were used. The operation was delayed a little beyond the scheduled date of March 2, and it was sunset on the 4th when the boats arrived safely at French Frigate Shoal from Jaluit. Having fueled from the submarines, the flying boats left for Hawaii, attacked Pearl Harbor seven hours after sunset, and returned safely to Jaluit in one hop.

On the same day an enemy task force attacked Wake Island, and in consequence the second attack by flying boats was postponed to a day subsequent to March 5. This operation, however, was canceled and the submarines were ordered to take up positions to await the enemy task force on its return passage.

With the sudden development of the situation in the Solomon Islands in the early part of September, 1942,

---

* For further details see "Rendezvous in Reverse," in *U. S. Naval Proceedings,* May, 1953, p. 478.

and as soon as the decision was made for the 17th Army to launch the first general attack on Guadalcanal Island, Admiral Yamamoto, the C.-in-C. Combined Fleet, attempted to carry out an air reconnaissance with seaplanes over a wide area to the southeast of Guadalcanal Island. I-122 proceeded to the atoll in mid-September and was engaged in fueling flying boats for about one week. The flying boats carried out a reconnaissance of the enemy dispositions over a wide area and as a result it was possible for our forces to guard against unexpected enemy attacks.

Following the sea battles for the South Pacific, I-26 took part in the reconnaissance of areas to the south of the Solomons. She left Truk on October 5 and returned there on November 30, after spending several weeks in the Solomons area. During that time I-26 spent several days fueling the flying boats operating from Shortland base. In the course of these operations she grounded on a reef but was able to get off by lightening her tanks and going astern, though the three lower tubes were put out of action. On another occasion she was attacked by a B-17, but the damage suffered was negligible.

Enemy flying boats made frequent reconnaissance flights, but despite this danger I-122 was able to fuel flying boats at Indispensable Reef on the 10th of November. During the withdrawal from Guadalcanal, flying boats were still able to fuel at Indispensable Reef in January, 1943, but by early February the submarines were no longer able to carry out their task owing to enemy air attacks.

The U. S. offensive in the Solomons and eastern New Guinea was increasing in intensity day by day and the greater part of our submarine strength was employed in interrupting enemy reinforcements and carrying supplies to our own isolated advanced bases.

About mid-August, intelligence reports suggested that powerful U. S. forces were concentrating in Hawaii and preparing for the next operation. In order to confirm this, the Combined Fleet staff decided to send a submarine to Hawaii. I-36 was detailed for the purpose. She completed preparations and left Yokosuka early in September, 1943, arriving off Hawaii in mid-September. An air reconnaissance was attempted on September 20 and again on the 27th, but owing to the efficiency of U. S. radar, close approach was difficult. The operation had to be abandoned, for it was impossible to launch and recover the aircraft far out to sea. Further attempts to approach also failed, and by mid-October the captain of the boat was desperate. Eventually the reconnaissance was carried out by launching the aircraft out at sea in a position three hundred miles from Hawaii, so that its range allowed only a one-way flight.

The aircraft reported four battleships, four aircraft carriers, five cruisers, and seventeen destroyers in Pearl Harbor, and failed to return. The next day the submarine fell in with a large convoy on a southeasterly course in a position three hundred miles southwest of Pearl Harbor and went in pursuit. On receiving I-36's report, the C.-in-C. Combined Fleet immediately dispatched I-35, 19, 169, and 175 to the Hawaiian area, but soon afterward contact with the convoy was lost. Later on the lost convoy suddenly appeared off the Gilberts, on November 19, and the submarines were ordered to concentrate in this area.

A number of the latest types of submarine had been added to the special operation units which returned from Hawaii, and the 8th Submarine Squadron was formed with eight boats: I-18, 20, 21, 22, 24, 27, 29, and 30. These carried out training in preparation for the second period of special operations under the command of Rear Admiral Ishizaki. At the end of April, 1942, I-10, 16, 18, 20, and 30 sailed for the Indian Ocean via Penang and carried out a reconnaissance of important points on the African coast. As a result it was decided to carry out an attack on Diégo-Suarez on May 31. The previous day I-10's aircraft reported one *Queen Elizabeth*-class battleship, one cruiser, and other ships at anchor in Diégo-Suarez. At midnight on the 30th, midget submarines carried by I-16 and 20 were launched from a point ten miles from the harbor entrance. I-18 failed to launch her midget owing to a breakdown of the engines. Both submarines waited at the recovery point and searched until June 2, but neither craft returned. It was only afterward that we learned that the *Queen Elizabeth*-class battleship had been badly damaged,* and that after the attack the crews of the midgets had landed, fought, and been killed.

---

* HMS *Ramillies* suffered one torpedo hit. She proceeded back to Durban with one compartment flooded. The other midget submarine sank a large tanker.

Another section of the 8th Submarine Squadron comprising submarines I-22, 24, 27, 21, and 29, under the command of Captain Sasaki, were operating in Australian waters during the latter part of May, 1942. A battleship, a cruiser, and other units were observed at anchor in Sydney harbor. The aircraft from I-21 confirmed the presence of these vessels on May 29, and it was decided to attack on the 31st. Accordingly, midget submarines were launched from submarines I-22, 24, and 27 from a position seven miles east of Sydney at 4:30 P.M. on May 31. Two of the submarines' aircraft had been damaged and it was not possible to observe the result, but it was ascertained after the war that one torpedo passed the stern of a cruiser and exploded between it and a quay, damaged a motorboat, and caused minor damage to the cruiser, but the results achieved by the other two boats are not clear.* Though the results achieved were meager, a great element of surprise was achieved by carrying out a midget attack inside the harbor of Sydney, Australia's greatest city. In later years, when the war had taken a difficult turn for us, the spirit displayed by those who were killed in action at Sydney was an example which insured ample volunteers for crews for these special units.

---

* U. S. sources record that out of four midgets launched, one became entangled in the nets across the harbor entrance. Three got through. One fired a torpedo which narrowly missed USS *Chicago* and USS *Perkins*. The *Chicago* is believed to have fired on and sunk one of the midgets before she and the *Perkins* took to the open sea. The Australian cruiser *Canberra* remained in her berth unharmed. Of the other two midgets, one was sunk by the harbor patrol and the other blew up when her torpedo jammed and exploded.

In view of the scale of enemy patrol activity in the vicinity of Lunga anchorage, it was decided to carry out a midget submarine attack inside the anchorage, with a unit comprising I-16, 20, and 24 under the command of Captain N. Ota. The plan was to embark the midgets at Truk or Shortland and to proceed to the northern entrance of Indispensable Strait and launch the midgets as necessary. After the attack the midgets were to return to Marovovo on the northern extremity of Guadalcanal, where the crews were to land, after having sunk their boats. Submarines I-16 and 20 attacked on November 15, 1942, sinking a transport and a destroyer, but only one midget returned.

I-16 and 20 each made two midget launches during the period from mid-November to mid-December, sinking two transports and one destroyer, and two other vessels were seen to sink from shore, making a total of five ships. One midget couldn't fire its torpedo due to a breakdown. Half the midget submarines failed to return.

In the Philippines four midget submarines were stationed at Cebu, two at Zamboanga, and two at Davao to defend the San Bernardino and Surigao straits in the center of Mindanao. The enemy invasion of the Philippines was developing, and as traffic was increasing between Mindanao and the Sulu Sea the area selected for the attack was in the narrowest part, between the southern tip of Negros Island and the northern tip of Mindanao Island. The units were standing by to come out from Dumaguete, on reports from the lookout station at Surigao. Between December 8 and March 21, 1945, fourteen vessels were sunk by this force, including two cruisers, one seaplane carrier, five destroyers, five transports, and some others. On March 20, 1945, the American forces landed at Davao, making the base untenable, so the midget crews scuttled their craft and landed to take part in the fight.

4

BOMBARDMENT

BY SUBMARINE

Our submarines were normally armed with guns ranging in size from 8- to 14-cm., either flat-trajectory or high-angle types, with twin-barrel 25-mm. machine guns for antiaircraft purposes. Most nations were agreed that such armament was effective for engaging unarmed merchantmen or targets ashore in areas unequipped with shore batteries. Submarine armaments were never intended for coping with warships or areas in which there were shore batteries. In a submarine, which might need over a minute from the time of surfacing to take aim and open fire, there was always the anxiety that the enemy would get the range and fire first. Furthermore, our submarine range-finders were mostly of the portable type, and consequently inaccurate. Thus methods of firing were very primitive, and it was liable to be a considerable time before a hit was obtained.

Up to about twenty rounds of ammunition were stored in a locker on the upper deck, and any required over and above this number had to be brought up from the magazine. This arrangement had the disadvantage of increasing the time taken in submerging in a crash dive. since the lid of the ammunition hoist could not be closed effectively from inside the boat. There was no way of stopping an influx of water if the lid was not properly closed. Moreover, and this is most important, a submarine proceeding on the surface in a state of readiness for submerging can well be sunk by machine-gun attack. For these reasons our submarines could resort to using their guns only in limited circumstances. Thus it happened that the gunnery officer of a submarine was usually only a young sublieutenant.

For those boats carrying a high-angle gun it was impossible, except by sheer luck, to obtain a hit on an aircraft unless one was equipped with the latest fire-control installation. As a gunnery officer of a submarine, I myself have tried to score a hit on an aircraft with a single high-angle gun, but never succeeded, for the range was estimated by eye and the shots fired at random. Radar enables an accurate range to be obtained, but our submarines were not equipped with gunnery radar even by the end of the war. In actual fact there were few occasions in the late war when submarines engaged aircraft. Any submarine which sighted aircraft some distance off would dive, and it was only when this was impossible that she would engage the aircraft by gunfire. Once, in 1944, when submarine I-44 was being harassed by an enemy flying boat off Admiralty Island, she elected to remain on the surface and engaged the aircraft with her low-angle gun. She was fortunate to reach base safely.

From the beginning of the war until January, 1943, most of our submarines which carried out bombardments on a variety of enemy territories were able to make their escape under cover of darkness and avoid any counterattack. The ranges were mostly calculated by means of the distance on the chart from the ship's position to the target. The position of the fall of shot of the first round was thus somewhat problematical in view of the inevitable errors involved. Therefore it was quite useless to aim for a small target, and the usual practice was to plaster a particular area with the idea of frightening the populace. Actually, orders to carry out a bombardment were not popular with submarine captains, though to the uninitiated the task might have appeared rather a stirring exploit. A counterattack might spell the doom of the submarine and even a single hit might make the boat unfit for diving. The boat could, of course, approach her target unseen under the surface in waters where an attack by surface vessels would have been impossible. Though the ensuing bombardment might not arouse excessive publicity, it was clearly unwise to repeat such an operation in the same area, so that for success both accuracy and good fortune were essential. However, in spite of this, there were instances when submarine bombardment achieved the destruction by fire of barracks and other important targets.

The attacks on Johnston Island, carried out by submarines I-22 and 16 on about December 16, 1941, were the first land bombardments of their kind. This island is about a thousand yards long and two hundred and fifty yards wide. The coast is mountainous, and indeed there is little flat ground anywhere on the island, which was being used as a flying-boat base. When submarine I-22 approached, it was cloudy, no observations could be taken, and her position could not be assessed accurately. Suddenly the island was sighted at the short range of a thousand yards, and the bombardment was carried out after sunset. I-16 failed to find the target. Later, I-68 of the 3rd Submarine Squadron attacked the island by gunfire. One submarine of the 3rd Squadron bombarded Palmyra at the end of December, 1941. In the resultant confusion she ran aground but got away without damage.

Hawaii, Maui, and Kauai were also bombarded about this time by ships of the 2nd Submarine Squadron.

On December 10 and 11, 1941, the obsolete submarines RO-13, 64, and 68, using 8-cm. guns, destroyed enemy flying-boat installations on Howland and

Baker islands in the Central Pacific. Early in 1942 they took part in attacks on the U. S. mainland.

During the latter half of January, 1942, I-24 and 18 were ordered to bombard Midway Island, but only I-24 succeeded. At the beginning of February, I-169 fired on military establishments on Sand Island, after completing a watching patrol on Midway. In June, 1942, the island was again attacked by I-168.

On February 24, 1942, submarine I-17 penetrated the Santa Barbara Straits to the north of Los Angeles, and made the first submarine bombardment of America itself. The boat surfaced five minutes before sunset and fired rapidly at a target indicated by the captain at the periscope. There was evidence of panic on shore. Air-raid sirens were sounded. After firing ten rounds, I-17 retired at high speed on the surface. En route she met an enemy destroyer hurrying to the scene of action, but slipped by unnoticed.

At the end of June, submarine I-26 fired on the Naval Wireless Navigational Station at Vancouver Island. The enemy telegraphed an SOS, extinguished the lamps in the lighthouse, and darkened the area amid great confusion. Although seventeen rounds were fired, only slight damage was caused.

Submarine I-25 was given the task of bombarding the submarine base at Astoria. She approached the coast submerged, and surfaced in the moonlight to find herself in the middle of a pearling fleet. She dived again with great dispatch! The operation was postponed until the next day, when again I-25 approached and surfaced.

It was full moon and a fine night. This time there was no other vessel in sight. Twenty rounds were fired at shore targets. Again sirens sounded, while much confusion reigned.

Though damage resulting from these submarine bombardments was perhaps slight, operations continued throughout the year. In March I-4 attacked Cocos Island. This island was attacked again by I-166 in January, 1943, at the time of the withdrawal operations from Guadalcanal. At the same time, submarine I-165 attacked Port Gregory to the north of Geraldton, on the west coast of Australia. The cruiser *Nara*, a destroyer, and submarine I-8 fired on Canton Island to provide a diversion during the withdrawal from Guadalcanal.

On August 31 the flying-boat base in Graciosa Bay in the Solomons was fired on by I-19 from outside the bay. This caused little damage, so on September 8 submarine I-31 boldly entered the bay and successfully repeated the attack, causing appreciable damage.

During mid-October, 1942, submarine I-7 attacked the aerodrome on Espiritu Santo Island. Later the same boat repeated the attack, causing enough damage to considerably limit the movements of enemy aircraft during the general attack on Guadalcanal.

Australia, too, was chosen for attack. The steel works and shipyards at Newcastle were bombarded on June 7 and 8 by submarine I-21, while I-24, after launching her midgets off Sydney, surfaced at the entrance to Sydney Bay and fired over ten rounds in the direction of the city at a range of some six miles. Up till that moment the city lights were reflected brightly in the sky, but after the first round they suddenly went out. Simultaneously searchlights blazed out over the bay, illuminating the submarine clearly. However, she was able to dive and escape.

Another part played by gunfire in submarine warfare was the sinking of merchant ships already crippled by torpedoes. This was desirable as a means of economizing in torpedoes, but it involved much expenditure of ammunition and time in waters subject to alert enemy patrols, and there was seldom sufficient time to sink ships by such a relatively leisurely method. Indeed, sometimes the merchantmen seemed virtually unsinkable.

In June, 1942, off Noumea, I-21 surfaced and attacked a merchant ship by gunfire in daylight. The crew took to the boats and made off. I-21 fired no less than sixty rounds, but still the ship wouldn't sink. On closer inspection it was found that she was holed only above the waterline.

In May, 1942, at Dutch Harbor, I-26 had a similar experience. The submarine's gun got hot, but still the merchant ship wouldn't sink. After firing fifty rounds, the captain sank the ship by torpedo.

Tankers were always very difficult to sink. Reports by submarine captains operating off the west coast of America at the beginning of the war stated that these ships would not sink, however many torpedoes were fired: they just remained stopped. Hit after hit was registered with torpedoes by one submarine, but the tanker continued to float, and in the end all six torpedoes were fired from all the tubes. When this failed to sink the tanker, the submarine surfaced and attacked by gunfire, and she in turn was fired on and had to make off. It was generally accepted that no tanker could be disposed of unless both torpedoes and gunfire were used.

5

DESTRUCTION

OF COMMERCE

(*See Appendix B, p. 255*)

In World War I, Germany adopted the policy of sinking at sight without warning in an effort to force the Allies, and particularly England, into submission. This was unrestricted submarine warfare, and in World War II, Germany, after much research into the matter, adopted the same line, but this, too, ended in failure.

The United States adopted these tactics against Japan and achieved great success by concentrating her main effort with submarines on severing lines of communication.

The Japanese policy was to use submarines primarily for attacking enemy naval forces. Attacks on merchant shipping had only second priority. Thus enemy aircraft carriers were the chief target, then battleships and other naval craft. Merchant ships were legitimate targets only when there were no warships to be considered. Throughout the war destruction of commerce was undertaken only when the fighting strength of the fleet allowed.

Submarine I-6 was in the Kauai Channel to the southeast of Pearl Harbor on December 10, 1941, and received a report: "Two cruisers and *Lexington*-class aircraft carrier on the northeasterly course." The admiral, commanding the 6th Fleet in his flagship *Katori* at Kwajalein base in the Marshall Islands, immediately ordered pursuit by submarines of the 1st Submarine Squadron comprising I-9 (Senior Officer), 15, 17, 19, 21, 23, and 25, which was stationed to the north of Oahu Island. Orders were also given to submarines I-10 and 26 to "stand by." These were stationed on the route between Hawaii and the American mainland, where they patrolled, alert, awaiting the appearance of the aircraft carrier, but nothing was sighted. The hunt was continued to a point near the American coast. When it became clear that the quarry had escaped, this unit was instructed to attack merchant shipping in this area. By then the force included submarines I-26, 25, 9, 17,

15, 23, 21, 19, and 10, and among them they ranged from off Seattle in the north to Los Angeles in the south. These were the latest submarines then available, with a displacement of two thousand tons—carrying an aircraft and having a surface speed of twenty-four knots. I-9 and 10 were special larger types.

They continued to operate against merchant ships during the latter half of December, but at about this time there was a great increase in the efficiency of American patrols. During this period about ten tankers and cargo ships were sunk. Submarine I-26 on the northern end of the patrol had left on operations immediately after her reconstruction and like I-24, in which I was serving prior to the outbreak of war, had carried out practically no working-up program, and in consequence suffered a series of defects. After carrying out a patrol in the Aleutians just prior to the war, she was stationed between Hawaii and San Francisco at the outbreak of hostilities. On the morning of December 8, I-26 sank a three-thousand-ton-class military transport by gunfire, scoring the first kill by a Japanese submarine in the war. She then proceeded to the vicinity of Vancouver, where she fired a torpedo at a merchant ship, but missed. According to the prewar battle instructions, the numbers of torpedoes to be fired at various targets were rigidly fixed, i.e., merchant ships and destroyers—one torpedo; cruisers—three; battleships and aircraft carriers—all available tubes. This limited the chances of hitting a merchant ship rather severely, for it must be remembered that a torpedo does not run as accurately as a shell fired from a gun. Various trials had shown that a hit could be expected at the short range of about eight hundred yards, but outside this a hit with one torpedo would be very doubtful.

On about December 27 submarine I-25, commanded by Commander Tagami, approached to within ten miles of the Columbia River entrance and, surfacing in dark and rainy conditions, torpedoed the twenty-thousand-ton ship *Connecticut* and brought her to a stop. She didn't seem to be sinking and the captain was about to fire a second torpedo when she started to go down. The crew got away in boats and, according to the American radio, landed safely on shore.

Submarine I-23, under Commander Nashida, opened fire with her gun at an old gunboat on the surface in daylight, but failed to obtain many hits. On pursuit the gunboat made for Monterey Bay, and her rudder was hit, causing her to go round in circles, much to the consternation of those watching on shore. Eventually the gunboat ran aground and, having given her a few more rounds, the submarine put to sea.

At the end of December the submarines left the American coast and by mid-January had arrived at the base at Kwajalein in the Marshalls. While submarine I-25 was on passage between Johnston Island and the Marshalls, she picked up some enemy signals on her D/F set and proceeded along the requisite bearing. Just before sunset on January 8 the gunnery officer, Sublieutenant Takahashi, who was on watch, reported, "Island in sight."

Further inspection suggested that it was not an island but a warship. The captain immediately dived the boat and made the approach with all tubes at the ready. Periscope inspection revealed what now seemed to be a seaplane carrier. The flight deck and derricks could be seen, with five aircraft ranged on deck. She had stopped when the submarine got sufficiently close to have a good look. With a smile on his face, the captain fired four torpedoes, all of which hit.*

After these operations against merchant shipping, I-8 left Kwajalein on a similar patrol at the end of January, and arrived west of San Francisco in early February. She cruised as far north as Seattle but had no opportunities for attack and returned to Japan at the beginning of March. Submarine I-17, with a companion vessel, set out in search of an enemy task force which attacked Kwajalein anchorage on February 2, but failed to make any contact and carried on to the west coast of North America, arriving off San Diego on February 20. After the bombardment of Santa Barbara, already described, I-17 sank a merchant ship by torpedo off San Francisco, but was fired on when surfacing after the attack. It seemed that the enemy had already armed its merchantmen. Subsequently I-6 sank another merchant ship before returning to home waters at the end of March. After this, the attack on shipping off the American coast was temporarily abandoned, but on her return passage from attacking the Oregon coast with incendiaries, I-25 carried out some attacks at the northern sector of the American coastline in early October, when she sank two tankers. Continuing to search for targets, she was

---

* This claim has not been substantiated by Allied sources.

herself attacked by American bombers at a most inopportune moment, for everyone, including the engineroom staff, was out on deck smoking. The bombs fell when she had submerged to a depth of only twenty feet. Luckily, damage was confined to the aerial, which was destroyed, causing a leak. It became impossible to transmit messages, but nevertheless she continued on patrol. Next, while cruising to the north of Seattle, she sighted what looked like a warship's mast. This proved to be two U. S. submarines on a southeasterly course. There was only one torpedo left. This was fired after closing in to five hundred yards. The torpedo scored a hit, and one American submarine sank after a loud explosion, but owing to the nearness of the vessel, the violent concussion sprang all I-25's rivets.

At the end of May, 1942, in anticipation of the Aleutian and Midway operations, submarines I-25 and 26 proceeded to the vicinity of Seattle via the Aleutians, and while on patrol at the entrance to Straits of Vancouver, sank one merchant ship. In 1943 all units were fighting in the Solomons, and there is nothing to record from the American area. Some results were achieved in this area in 1944, and I-12 sank two ships toward the end of that year, but all news of this submarine ceased after January, 1945.

These operations off the American coast, though only on a restricted scale, were thus not unsuccessful.

The Indian Ocean provided another operational area. After the fall of Penang in the Malay Peninsula into Japanese hands, our submarines proceeded, in January, 1942, into the Indian Ocean without waiting for the fall of Singapore, and began their attacks on merchant ships.

Up until 1944 the scale of enemy convoys in that area was light, and while the number of our submarines so employed varied according to circumstances, attacks on merchant shipping were maintained throughout the period. Although under the terms of our agreement with Germany, some changes in the situation occurred from time to time, generally the area of operations assigned to Japanese submarines extended from the Arabian Sea to South Africa and covered the whole of the Indian Ocean. Our losses were small and the harvest large, while in the Pacific it was just the other way round. As a result, all submarine captains preferred operating in the Indian Ocean. I must confess that I myself hoped to be sent to this area, but unfortunately the chance did not materialize. Compared with the bases in the southern seas, Penang was better equipped in every way and was very popular with submarine crews, and the Indian Ocean campaign was regarded almost as a paradise compared with the "Hell War" in the Pacific. The sinking of unescorted merchant ships presented no difficulty. The more venturesome submarine captains would go alongside the enemy vessels and set fire to them with petrol, thus economizing in shells and torpedoes. The majority of these captains later met their end in the Pacific. Appendix B gives a list of the eighty vessels sunk in the Indian Ocean for the loss of only two Japanese submarines—I-160 and 34. I-160 was sunk by a British destroyer in the Sunda Straits and the other by a British submarine at the entrance to Penang when en route to Japan in November, 1943.

One of the most notable operations was that carried out by units of the 8th Submarine Squadron in the Mozambique Channel during two separate periods, extending over three months. All units returned safely to Penang at the beginning of August. Two raiding vessels, *Hokoku Maru* and *Aikoku Maru*, equipped with torpedo tubes, operated with the submarines. As well as acting as fuel tankers for the submarines, they captured one vessel and sank another.

In 1944, too, although the situation in the Pacific was deteriorating, destruction of merchant shipping in the Indian Ocean continued, but the scale of enemy convoys increased, the numbers of available submarines gradually fell, and our losses began to mount. On February 11, 1944, RO-110 was sunk in action with an Allied gunboat off Vizagapatam (Bay of Bengal) and all news of I-27 ceased in February of the same year.

In September, 1944, I-8, 37, 165, RO-113, and 115 were stationed in the Indian Ocean, but toward the end of the year these vessels were gradually withdrawn to take part in the Pacific war, and within six months all were lost in that area.

Submarine I-6 successfully laid magnetic mines from her torpedo tubes in the vicinity of Brisbane. We learned about these mines from the Germans. Two or three were carried in each tube and, when dropped at suitable intervals, they sank to the bottom. Submarines

I-121, 122, 123, and 124 were specially equipped for mine-laying duties. In addition to the bow tubes, the stern of the boat was specially adapted for laying mines. They were normally styled "mine-laying submarines," with a displacement of over one thousand tons and a surface speed of fourteen knots—and were an obsolete type of vessel completed about 1925-27. In 1940 they were equipped with petrol tanks on the upper deck for refueling aircraft, and were thus able to carry out an additional role. Their peculiar construction made them very difficult boats to handle. Their surface speed was slow and they were difficult to maneuver submerged, owing to their small hydroplanes and rudders. The slightest difference in weight forward or aft gave them a list. If the least bit lightened they tended to surface and if made overheavy they tended to sink. They were known throughout the service as the "dreaded submarines."

I served as torpedo officer of one of these craft in 1940. When a mine was dropped, a compensatory weight of water had to be let in, otherwise the stern would break surface. If too much water were let in, the boat would sink. The forty-eight mines had to be moved one by one to the tail of the boat, while water was pumped to the fore-end to prevent the boat from becoming tail-heavy—a really dangerous task. Some accidents due to faulty procedure were reported, including casualties caused by the sudden movement of mines due to bad trimming. Personally I was fortunate enough to avoid being responsible for any mishaps, thanks to the skill of our coxswain, who had had six years' service in submarines. It was extremely difficult to keep the boat level and at the prescribed depth and at the same time lay the mines in the correct positions. Usually the mines had to be laid with a two-knot tide running at the entrance to bays, and very careful cooperation between captain and navigator was necessary to avoid any dangerous error.

On December 1, just before the outbreak of war, the mine-laying unit assembled at Hainan Island left harbor. Forty mines were laid secretly on December 8 by I-123 in the western entrance to the Balabac Strait, and by I-124 off Manila. After completing this task, I-124 rescued aircraft crews who had crashed in the air attack on Manila, and was also engaged in sending out weather reports. Submarines I-121 and 122 laid mines in the Singapore Channel and sank a merchant ship escaping from this area on December 10. I-123 subsequently laid mines at the northern entrance to the Surabaya Strait and I-121 made another visit to Manila Bay, but was unable to lay mines because of the vigilance of enemy patrols. In addition, submarine I-6 laid mines from her torpedo tubes as previously related.

In June, 1942, it was planned to try to weaken the resolve of the enemy to fight by carrying out large-scale commerce destruction in the Indian Ocean and Australian areas, and also with the idea of wiping out the effect of defeat of Midway. However, the enemy chose this moment for his counterattack in the Solomons and most of our submarines had to concentrate in this area to counteract this.

Nevertheless, small forces continued to operate in the Indian Ocean and Australian areas, and the 8th Submarine Squadron proceeded with these operations on completion of the midget attacks at Sydney and Diégo-Suarez.

In mid-June, after the battle of Midway, the 3rd Submarine Squadron, too, had commenced commerce destruction in the Australian area. I-24 attacked a merchant ship at night while off Sydney, but owing to a premature torpedo detonation, the merchant ship was able to make off at full speed. The captain of I-24 immediately gave the order to surface and engage by gunfire, but with no searchlight it was difficult to score a hit in the pitch dark.

Eventually one round did hit, which stopped the ship, and the crew took to the boats. I-24 was then able to sink the vessel by torpedo, but intercepted an SOS from the doomed ship saying she was being attacked by a submarine and asking for assistance. There were other instances of premature detonations and these were due to oversensitive fuses, which were afterward remedied. In this particular instance, the captain hesitated before using any further torpedoes, but is said to have sunk two more ships.

After our withdrawal from Guadalcanal, enemy patrols became more vigilant and our losses increased. This was due in part to the development by the enemy of warning devices and also to the enemy's control in the air, as our own carrier-aircraft strength declined. Furthermore, enemy transports were using the inside of the Great Barrier Reef off the northeast coast of Australia, where antisubmarine precautions were very strict, so that little success was achieved in cutting off the enemy's supply routes to the rear in the Guadalcanal and New Guinea areas, although it was reputed for a time that aircraft in Australia were without petrol. Generally, the situation seemed to be turning against us. The 6th Fleet H.Q. at the submarine base on Truk Island viewed matters with increasing concern.

.

6

SUBMARINE

COMMUNICATION

BETWEEN JAPAN

AND GERMANY

Since the vast territories between Japan and Germany were all hostile, the only means of communication was by the long sea route across the Indian Ocean, round the Cape of Good Hope to the Atlantic, and so to Occupied France. This was the route followed by the Russian Baltic Fleet during the Russo-Japanese War, a distance of over fifteen thousand miles. The difficulties en route were very great, and a constant source of worry. In addition to enemy submarines, aircraft, and patrol craft, the track passed through the "Roaring Forties," and there were many changes in climate. The hardships in the cold weather were almost unbearable. It is not surprising therefore that out of five boats, only one made the return voyage without mishap. Several German submarines came to Singapore and also to Japan itself. Indeed, Admiral Nomura returned to the home country in a German submarine. A number of Japanese army officers planned their liaison trips by German submarine, but few returned safely to Japan and all made their wills before leaving Berlin for the return journey.

Submarine I-30 (Commander S. Endo) was the first to be selected for the voyage to Germany. After taking part in the midget submarine operation at Diégo-Suarez, this submarine, having fueled and taken in supplies from the raiders *Hokoku Maru* and *Aikoku Maru*, left her consorts and proceeded independently via the Cape of Good Hope. Being the beginning of July, it was exceedingly rough in the "Roaring Forties," but she got through and entered the Bay of Biscay on August 2. Three days later she was met by German mine sweepers and arrived at Lorient the same day. Having exchanged equipment and other commodities, the captain was decorated with a German medal and the boat set out on her return journey, arriving back at Singapore in October, 1942. But on her departure from that port, she struck a British mine and sank, and much valuable material was lost, though most of her crew were saved.

At the end of June, 1943, submarine I-8 completed preparations for a long trip. She was to take to Brest a crew whose job it would be to bring back to Japan the submarine RO-501, built in Germany for the Japanese submarine fleet. As a present for the Germans, I-8 took a cargo of quinine.

In company with I-10, she sailed from Penang on July 6, under the command of Captain Shinji Uchino. The first part of the journey across the Indian Ocean was uneventful and was accomplished in reasonable comfort, for the swell usually affecting these waters was absent.

Refueling from I-10 was carried out according to plan, and I-8 proceeded on her way round the Cape of Good Hope. To avoid enemy patrols expected in the vicinity, I-8's course lay some three hundred miles off the cape, through an area where the "Roaring Forties" are said to extend over a thousand-mile belt. For ten days she battled with tremendous seas, unable to do more than five knots. The upper deck and bridge were damaged and the aircraft hangar swayed so much as the water swept over that eventually it shifted bodily. Twice, members of the crew, secured by lifelines, effected repairs in the teeth of the gale.

Eventually, calmer waters were reached and I-8 was able to continue on her way, making for the Bay of Biscay. As she headed north of the West African coast, she had to keep well clear of the U. S. air base in the Azores. At an appointed rendezvous just south of the Azores she made contact with a German U-boat and in the space of four hours the Germans had equipped I-8 with radar search gear, without which the dangers of sudden air attack would have been very great; the Japanese radar equipment originally fitted had proved useless. Personnel from the U-boat rowed over to I-8 in a rubber dinghy—a somewhat old-fashioned method of communication—but the operation was carried out safely and I-8 went on her way again, setting course for Brest.

In the Bay of Biscay, passing five miles off the Spanish coast, it was necessary to remain submerged to avoid merchant ships and the undesired attention of enemy aircraft. Enemy patrols were very alert at the entrance to the bay, but German aircraft came out in support.

Nearer Brest this escort was augmented by more aircraft and ten German destroyers, while torpedo boats swept a passage through the magnetic mines into harbor.

On September 5, I-8 slipped through the last protected entrance and into the U-boat bunker. There she lay roofed over with some twenty feet of reinforced concrete, immune from air attack at last, after her sixty-one days' voyage from Penang.

In the German submarine bases the repair shops and the accommodation were all protected in this way, so that whatever the scale of air attack, boats could be repaired and crews rested in complete safety. By contrast, conditions in the major naval ports in Japan were lamentable; every air attack was the occasion of much confusion.

By mid-September, I-8 prepared to sail on her return voyage. Several hundred tons of material needed in Japan were taken on board. Even the torpedo tubes were filled. The cargo included machinery for torpedoes, four-barrel machine guns, machine guns for aircraft, and deck watches (those made in Japan were inaccurate and unsuitable for astronomical observations).

I-8 sailed under strong escort. As a safety measure, it was decided that after the escort had bidden farewell and left I-8 to proceed alone, communication between the submarine and the German Navy would be restricted to three signals sent by W/T:

"Passed position A," indicating "Left greatest danger area,"

"Passed position B," indicating "Crossed the equator," and

"Passed position C," meaning "Left Atlantic."

Position A was passed and reported. As I-8 crossed the equator, heading south, thinking all was safe, she duly signaled "Passed position B." The next day an enemy aircraft appeared. It seemed that the message had given the enemy a D/F bearing. I-8 dived quickly and escaped, but the following morning, when she was on the surface, she was attacked by an enemy plane. As she was diving deep to the one-hundred-and-eighty-foot mark, the plane dropped its bombs. The lights in the submarine grew dim. Water was reported to be entering the crew's quarters. For a moment it seemed that the end had come, but soon the inrush of water was traced to a leaky valve. The defect was rectified speedily, and further inspection proved that, after all, little damage had been sustained. Everyone relaxed. But she remained submerged for the rest of the day.

In the "Roaring Forties" rough weather smashed the

glass on the bridge, but otherwise on the return voyage there was no damage to the upper deck. In this area I-8 remained submerged during daylight for two successive days, to avoid being spotted in the vicinity of enemy bases. Afterward she was able to proceed on the surface, and though she was buffeted by gales as on the outward journey, the wind was somewhat less severe.

In the Indian Ocean it was deemed safe to affix identity marks. In the midst of this operation an aircraft appeared and swooped down on the submarine as it lay on the surface. Fortunately it was a friendly plane.

By the time she entered the Indian Ocean, fuel was running low. Signals were sent off to Penang base and to Japanese units in the Indian Ocean. There was no reply, so I-8 continued on her journey, passing through the Sunda Strait and reaching Singapore early in December. The return passage thus took sixty-four days. Later I-8 reached Japan safely. She was the only Japanese submarine to accomplish the round trip of thirty thousand miles.

The German passengers carried on the return voyage were three naval officers, four radar and hydrophone technicians, a German army major, and four civilians. Thanks to German foresight, the food was mostly rice, probably grown in Italy and southern France. At first the Germans ate one Japanese meal every day, but after about ten days they all asked for bread instead.

Submarine I-29 (Commander T. Kinashi), having received orders to contact a German submarine in the

Indian Ocean, left Penang in early April, 1943. Proceeding through the Mozambique Channel, she met the German submarine four hundred miles south-southwest of Madagascar on April 28. Here she embarked Chandra Bose, the leader of the Indian Independence Movement, and, one of his companions, and, after transferring an officer destined for Germany, she proceeded on the return voyage, reaching Penang early in May. The successful accomplishment of this voyage gave an impetus to the Indian Independence Movement and damped down the idea of an Allied offensive in the Indian area.

I-29 was later employed in attacking shipping in the Indian Ocean; early in November, 1943, she sailed again from Penang, this time bound for Germany. Following the same route as I-30 and 8, she arrived safely on the west coast of France. On the return journey, between Singapore and Japan, she was torpedoed by a U. S. submarine in the Bashi Channel off southern Formosa. The captain and most of the crew perished.

In 1943, I-34 completed preparations in Japan for a voyage to Germany and then spent a week at Singapore, loading rubber, tin, tungsten, and quinine. On November 11 she sailed from Singapore and proceeded through the Strait of Malacca. However, when almost in sight of Penang Island, and despite the strict lookout that was being kept, she was torpedoed and sunk by a British submarine.

Submarine RO-501, which had been built in Germany and was operated by a Japanese crew under the command of Commander Norida, started her voyage to Japan, but no news was received from her after she entered the Atlantic, and she was in fact sunk after being in action with a U. S. destroyer on May 13, 1944.

The last submarine to essay the trip, I-52 (Commander K. Uno) was a victim of the Normandy landings.*

Constructor-Commanders Hideo Tomonaga and M. Shoji, who had been working in Germany, received instructions to return to Tokyo in early 1945. It was arranged for them to take passage in a German submarine. Commander Tomonaga was a leading ship constructor, and Commander Shoji a first-rate technician in aircraft design. Their services were urgently required by the Japanese Navy. Details were arranged with the German naval authorities, and passengers and cargo were to be transferred to a Japanese submarine in the Indian Ocean. It was the end of January, 1945. Berlin, in a temperature of four or five degrees above zero, was nightly undergoing very heavy bombing raids. There were no electric light, no fuel, most of the windows were broken, and there were bitterly cold winds.

The Allied antisubmarine measures had recently increased in intensity and the Atlantic had become almost a graveyard for German submarines. Thus the passage of these officers in a German submarine was fraught

---

* According to Allied sources, I-52 was actually sunk by aircraft from the USS *Bogue* in the Atlantic Narrows, in a position 15° 16′ north, 39° 55′ west.

with great danger. The German U-boat failed to rendezvous with the Japanese submarine. Some weeks later, news of their fate was broadcast by a U. S. short-wave transmitter:

> While on patrol in the Gulf of Mexico a U. S. patrol craft captured a German submarine flying the white flag. The German captain and the crew were made prisoners and taken into custody ashore. The U. S. authorities who searched the interior of the boat discovered the bodies of two Japanese naval officers in uniform who had committed suicide by taking poison.

7

THE BATTLE

OF MIDWAY

The Battle of Midway took place on June 4, 1942. The Japanese Navy, excelling in carrier strength and flushed with victory after the Hawaiian àttack, was unaware that operational secrets had leaked out. And so we fell into the trap laid by the enemy, who was forewarned of our movements. A severe defeat ensued for the Japanese. Midway was a crucial battle which reversed the whole position in the Pacific war.

On June 6 a flying boat observed that the American carrier *Yorktown* had been abandoned. (The eventual destruction of this ship was the only success we achieved in the Battle of Midway.) Submarine I-168 (Commander Tanabe), which was in the vicinity, received an urgent signal to sink the carrier *Yorktown* in position one hundred and fifty miles to the northeast of Midway. All preparations for attack were made and I-168 proceeded at twenty-one knots to the position indicated. At about one o'clock on the morning of June 6, a black mass resembling a warship was sighted to the east. Daylight came. It was without doubt an aircraft carrier—with five or six destroyers circling round on guard.

I-168 approached, seeking a favorable position for breaking through the destroyer screen. She passed beneath the first line of destroyers undetected and came up to periscope depth. Inspection revealed the carrier was a little down by the stern, and this was confirmed on inspection from the opposite side. This was so remarkable that the captain made a closer inspection and found that the ship was in tow. Finally I-168 was able to get into position for attack. Four torpedoes were fired at 10 A.M., nine hours after the ship was first sighted. The rumbling sound of the explosion followed and a cry of exultation went up from those inside the submarine.

According to American sources made available after the war, two torpedoes hit the carrier and another hit the destroyer alongside, cutting it in two. The *Yorktown* turned over and sank the following day.

There was considerable reaction on the part of the destroyers guarding the *Yorktown*. In less than fifteen minutes after the incident, three destroyers began a depth-charge attack. I-168 suffered sixty near-misses, the worst of which lifted the boat almost a foot. The paint from the deck above came flaking down and the lights went out, leaving the boat in pitch darkness. The batteries were damaged and poisonous chlorine gas began to escape. Just when everyone thought the attack was over, another three depth charges exploded so close that they shook the boat. She lay crippled, unable to move, and with no pumps working. In order to remain submerged, water had to be taken in or expelled by air pressure. Work began at once to repair the lighting and isolate the damaged batteries. As it was impossible to use the trimming pumps, the boat was slanting upward at an angle of twenty degrees. It was just like being stranded halfway up a steep hill. But still there was hope. Working at this acute slope, the electricians had to be held in position by their mates, so that they did not slip. Efforts to bring the boat out on an even keel by moving men and foodstuffs forward were of no avail. Though there had been no fatal break nor inrush of water, the damage to the batteries was critical, for the main electrical supply was cut, leaving the boat without means of turning the propeller. The most vital task was to isolate the unusable battery and connect up the good ones. Although the crew had had much training in the operation of isolating a battery, the drill had not envisaged so large a break. In the dim light and with chlorine gas escaping steadily, it seemed the job would be impossible to finish, but at last the damaged battery was isolated and the stage was reached when the current was available again. Having inspected the connections to the motors, the chief electrician reported that he was satisfied. The switch was closed and the propeller started to move, the lights came on, and the hopes of all were realized.

The destroyers were still about overhead, so it was impossible to use the air pumps because of the noise they made. There was no compressed air for discharging the water, which was still coming in through the rear tubes, and it was therefore no longer possible to proceed submerged, so there was nothing else to do but to surface and fight it out with the enemy. There were three destroyers in sight at ten thousand yards. To add to the difficulties, acid was found leaking from the damaged batteries which once more suddenly ceased to function. On investigation it was found necessary to cut out more cells. Meanwhile the three destroyers had turned about, spotted the submarine, and were coming in to the attack. The range fell to five thousand yards. They came closer, firing their guns. It was essential to get even a little compressed air but enemy shells had begun to straddle the submarine, and the captain decided to submerge once more and lie still, for it would be dark in half an hour and in the darkness escape might still be possible. Hunting their quarry, the destroyers passed directly overhead, but after firing only a few depth charges they withdrew—perhaps they had no more left. The sound of their propellers grew less and finally ceased. At last repairs were completed and the lights came on again. It was 8 P.M., the sun had set and the sound of the enemy ships' propellers had entirely disappeared. I-168 surfaced thankfully and made off to the west and her home country at a speed of sixteen knots, making a detour to avoid an area ahead where star shells were being fired.

What were the other submarines doing during the important period of the Midway battle? One of them was to use French Frigate Shoal anchorage for the second Pearl Harbor reconnaissance operation. This was planned as before: the submarine to refuel the flying boat which would then attempt to observe the ships at anchor in Pearl Harbor. During the latter part of May, when the supply submarines I-21 and 23 came to reconnoiter French Frigate Shoal anchorage, they found that a U. S. seaplane carrier and other patrol craft were already there.

We also had I-171, 174, and 175 acting as wireless link ships and patrolling the area, but they had little opportunity to achieve anything. On May 25 they reported, "Patrols too alert, no prospects." They waited until May 31, but conditions were unchanged, so the operation was canceled and no knowledge was gained of the situation in Pearl Harbor. On this occasion the Americans had forestalled us by sending patrol craft to the spot.

Other plans, too, failed. Twelve vessels of the 3rd and 5th Submarine Squadrons comprising submarines I-168, 169, 171, 174, 175, 156, 157, 158, 159, 162, 165, and 166 (I-164 was sunk off Kyushu on May 17 and did not participate) left Kwajalein on May 25 and reached positions along the route between Pearl Harbor and Midway by June 6 in an attempt to catch the American reinforcements. The enemy, however, was forewarned of this plan, and so arranged that the task force passed the approaches to Midway earlier than originally scheduled. Thus we were left carrying on the pursuit from too far astern and not a single ship was sighted. We had no clear idea of the position of the task force, and in consequence, with the exception of I-168, we were unable to use our submarine strength in the Midway operations.

8

THE STRUGGLE

FOR GUADALCANAL

In 1942 the Japanese 4th Fleet, commanded by Vice-Admiral Inoue, carried out an attack on Port Moresby in an effort to gain complete control of New Guinea. The Fleet comprised the large aircraft carriers *Shokaku* and *Zuikaku*, the light carrier *Shoho*, cruisers, destroyers, and transports. The following submarine units were also included in the command:

21st Submarine Flotilla—Submarines RO-33 and 34.
8th Submarine Squadron, 11th Submarine Flotilla—Submarines I-29 and 28.
3rd Submarine Flotilla—Submarines I-22 and 24.

By the end of April submarines RO-33 and 34 had reconnoitered Russell Island and Deboyne anchorages, Jomard Channel, and the route to the east of Port Moresby, and investigated the presence or otherwise of the enemy in transport anchorages and shipping routes. Submarines I-22, 24, 28, and 29 reached their stations on May 5 but had no opportunities for attacking the enemy. Submarines RO-33 and 34 also failed to sight the enemy. Thus at the battle of the Coral Sea no positive results were obtained from submarines, and there were also no losses.

On August 7, 1942, the U. S. forces launched the first phase of their large-scale counterattack on Guadalcanal. The C.-in-C. 8th Fleet, Admiral Mikawa, himself led his cruiser force into action in the first naval battle of the Solomon Islands and achieved great success, but when he attacked a second time he was unable to cause any damage to the enemy landing operations or to his transports. The enemy not only held on to the airfield but gradually consolidated the defenses, and in the period between August, 1942, and February, 1943, when the Japanese forces withdrew from the island, there was much desperate fighting by land, sea, and air.

In the meantime our submarines were engaged in transporting supplies, attacking enemy transports, cutting off enemy reinforcements, refueling aircraft, or else watching for chances to attack enemy naval forces. Thus they all made a contribution to the heavy demands placed upon them. Unfortunately, this area was badly charted for friend and foe alike. There were cases of grounding on uncharted shoals, and operations were carried out under difficult conditions. Furthermore, the unceasing counterattacks by enemy aircraft and surface vessels doubled our losses. From about September, 1942, the efficiency of enemy radar equipment increased and our former supremacy, which had depended on the excellence of our binoculars, soon disappeared when it came to facing enemy aircraft on a dark night or in poor visibility. Night actions, operations where formerly we had excelled, now became difficult, and this also was a contributory cause to our mounting losses.

On August 7, on receipt of the report of the enemy landing on Guadalcanal Island, Admiral Mikawa immediately ordered all the submarines under his command to concentrate in Indispensable Strait. Submarines RO-34 and 33, I-121, 122, and 123 of the 7th Submarine Squadron proceeded to hunt for the enemy in Lunga and Tulagi anchorages. Submarine RO-33, after contacting the survivors on Guadalcanal Island and handing over medical supplies, sank an enemy transport in Lunga anchorage. This submarine was then continuously depth-charged over a distance of eighteen miles, but only its periscope was damaged. I-121 and 123 were ordered to bombard the enemy landing operations, and I-122 to search for the enemy in the Santa Cruz Islands area.

All surface vessels and all air units joined in the attack, and the submarines were redeployed off Guadalcanal Island and the area to the southeast of the Solomon Islands.

On August 24 submarines I-9, 15, 17, 19, 26, 31, and 33, which had hurried from Truk, arrived at the enemy dispersal lines between San Cristobal and Ndeni islands, and sighted an enemy task force.

I-26 had left Yokosuka on August 15 and arrived at the scene of action off the Solomons from Truk. To the northeast of the Solomons she sighted an enemy task force of an aircraft carrier, one battleship, a cruiser, and about ten destroyers. Attack was difficult, but she scored a hit on a *Lexington*-class carrier with one of her torpedoes.* After firing her torpedoes, I-26 was very close to the destroyers and therefore dived to three hundred feet. Four depth charges were dropped, but I-26 escaped damage.

From the end of December, 1942, submarines RO-100, 101, 102, and 103 were gradually organized into the 7th Submarine Squadron and were active in the vicinity of Rabaul. This class of submarine was the smallest in existence in Japan at the time and was intended for coastal defense. They were stationed mainly off Port Moresby, the area to the southeast of Milne Bay, the

---

* This was the *Saratoga*. After firing six torpedoes, I-26 came to periscope depth only thirty feet from the destroyer *McDonough's* bow. As she dived hurriedly she scraped the ship's hull! Even so I-26 survived and later in the year sank the American cruiser *Juneau*.

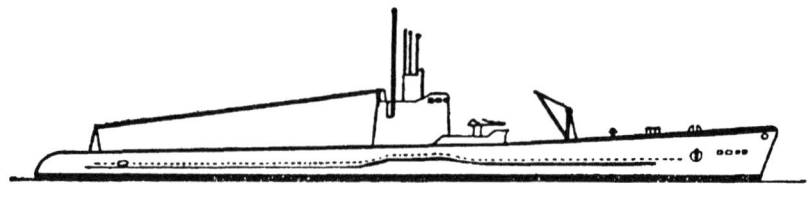

RO-100-class submarine. *See Appendix A (2).*

eastern portion of the Central Solomons, and the Jomard Channel, and at times carried out transport duties. By mid-August, 1943, the 7th Submarine Squadron had comprised submarines RO-34, 100, 101, 102, 103, 106, and 107, but had lost RO-34,* 102, 103, and 107, and had only the sinking of a transport by RO-106 in July to offset its own losses.

On April 1, 1943, a big counterattack (known as Operation I) was begun with combined naval and air forces under the personal command of Admiral Yamamoto, the C.-in-C. Combined Fleet; and attacks delivered in quick succession on April 7 achieved some success, but in face of the overwhelming air strength of the enemy it was just like throwing water on thirsty soil. At the beginning of May the Allied armies landed on Rendova in the New Guinea archipelago and began the westward advances in New Guinea. Against the landing operations at Rendova the Japanese Army put up stiff resistance with their forces on the spot and with reinforcements hurried from Rabaul, while a destroyer squadron and its flagship, a cruiser, carried out repeated counter-

---

* RO-34 was picked up by radar in the dark, small hours of April 5 and attacked on the surface by radar-controlled gunfire from U. S. destroyer *O'Bannon's* 5-inch guns and finally sunk at point-blank range with machine-gun fire and depth charges.

attacks, but their objectives were unobtainable in face of the pressure of enemy naval and air strength. In fact our forces were routed and suffered heavy losses. The RO-100-class submarines hurried to the scene of action. The RO-101, proceeding in advance, had been detailed to carry out her fourth trip to the western area of Guadalcanal and instructed to contain the landing and attack.

During September submarines RO-101,* 105, 106, and 109 concentrated their efforts on the area to the south and southeast of the Solomon group. Submarines RO-100, 104, and 108 were to attack the enemy in the Huon Bay area of eastern New Guinea. The direct results of these operations were nil—although submarine RO-105 succeeded in rescuing an air crew who had made a forced landing, but nothing further was heard of RO-101.

From mid-August, 1943, submarines RO-104, 105, 108, and 109 were reinforced and continued with the same assignments, but the task of counterattacking the enemy, who was landing anywhere at will, was completely hopeless.

Thus the RO-100-class submarines performed all manner of tasks—over a wide area—and had no opportunities for rest or refit. RO-108, operating in the Huon Bay area from the end of September, sighted and attacked three enemy destroyers fifty miles to the north of Cape Wardhunt on October 3. She was heavily depth-

---

* U. S. naval source reports RO-101 surprised on the surface at night and sunk by U. S. destroyer *Radford* on July 1, and was therefore not in action in September.

charged, but two of the destroyers were sunk. RO-106 and 109, operating in January in the Huon Bay area, sighted several enemy transports and escort craft, but had no chances of attacking. RO-105 likewise had no opportunities for attack in the Sulumi area.

RO-100 was sent on transport duty to Buin at the end of October owing to the critical situation on Bougainville Island. When thirty miles west of Oema Island, however, before arriving at Buin, she was sunk by torpedo on October 25.*

RO-104 and 105, while sailing to Sulumi with supplies during late October and early November, were ordered to help relieve the position in the Bougainville area and took part in the Bougainville area sea engagement, but had no successes to record, although they rescued the crews of the light cruiser *Sendai* and some crashed aircraft crews on November 2 and 6 respectively.

In early November our cruiser force was bombed by enemy aircraft after entering Rabaul; and as the other surface ships, too, were continuously being damaged by air attack, it was decided to withdraw *Chogei*, the flagship of the 7th Submarine Squadron, to home waters. The staff were landed and the admiral's flag was flown at the submarine base.

By the end of November the submarine strength consisted of four vessels, RO-104, 105, 100, and 109; in addition submarines I-38, 16, 6, and 117 were carrying out transport duties. Subsequently, Rabaul was totally un-

---

* According to official Allied sources, RO-100 was not sunk until November, 1944. See *also* Appendix C.

able to carry out its functions as a base owing to fierce enemy air attacks, and in the period up to March, 1944, when the 7th Submarine Squadron H.Q. was transferred to Truk, submarines RO-34, 100 (see footnote, p. 94), 102, 103, and 107 were sunk. This left only RO-104, 105, 108, and 199 to transfer when Rabaul, of many memories, was abandoned for Truk. To that date our losses in submarines in the Solomons, New Guinea, and Coral Sea area totaled twenty-five. Losses inflicted on the enemy included the aircraft carrier *Wasp*,* fourteen other ships sunk, and three badly damaged, but it must be remembered that the maximum effort was devoted to the supply of provisions, which brought no dividends in enemy losses.

---

* On September 15, 1942, I-19 hit the carrier *Wasp* with three out of four torpedoes, and I-15 hit the battleship *North Carolina* a few moments later.

According to British sources, it is possible that the *North Carolina* was hit by the same salvo which hit the *Wasp;* that is, by I-19, which is said to have fired a full salvo, and not four torpedoes only.

9

SUPPLIES

FOR THE

GUADALCANAL

GARRISON

In July, 1942, after graduating from the advanced course at the submarine school, I was given command of submarine RO-31 attached to the Yokosuka Command. We were busily engaged in training and in urgent trials and research, from which there was no respite.

One day a military truck loaded with bags of rice suddenly appeared at the wharf near the naval port, bringing a number of naval and military officials who requested us to try out firing bags of rice from the torpedo tubes! The situation at Guadalcanal Island made it dangerous for our submarines to hand over supplies when surfaced, so the idea was to eject them from the tubes when submerged.

We tried all sorts of schemes over a period of three days. Biscuit boxes were fired, but about a third of them were broken by the projections inside the torpedo tube and the all-too-precious rice was being scattered all over Tokyo Bay. Then we had the idea of stacking rice in rubber containers on deck and fitting a device to release them from inside the boat while submerged. Finally we tried firing the rice in a wooden container shaped like a torpedo, but the container broke up and likewise the bags of rice. We should have realized that this plywood torpedo was hopeless from the start in view of the high pressure necessary to fire it to overcome the water pressure; a weakened firing charge would have been insufficient to effect a proper discharge.

At the end of the trials the naval C.-in-C. at Yokosuka was obviously very moved when he spoke to us about the sorry plight of the garrison at Gudalcanal and the necessity for attempting such fantastic measures.

After the American attack on Guadalcanal on August 7, 1942, supplies had to be brought in by destroyers and submarines owing to the continued heavy losses in other surface vessels occasioned by the enemy's air superiority and our lack of airfields. In fact, after our defeat in the third general attack, there was no hope of recovering the aerodrome, and the garrison had to rely on submarines for supplies. A conference was held at Truk on board the submarine fleet flagship to discuss matters. All the senior officers of units and commanding officers of submarines were opposed to a plan which would virtually send the boats to their death merely for the sake of supply-landing, a purpose divorced from the normal functions of a submarine. However, the admiral commanding the submarine fleet announced that it was the Imperial Command that the troops on Guadalcanal Island were to be supplied at all costs. No further dissentient voices were heard. Thus our submarines became carriers, and the great majority, at that time dispersed patrolling the high seas, the Pacific, the Indian Ocean and the Australian waters, in search for targets in the shape of warships and merchant vessels, were recalled to the confined waters around Guadalcanal Island and were relegated to lying in wait, submerged, for enemy patrol craft and submarines. Each submarine had one gun removed and was left with only two torpedo tubes, a modification which, while giving them more space for carrying provisions, greatly reduced their offensive power.

Instructions issued by the C.-in-C. Combined Fleet on November 16, 1942, set out the plan to be followed.

Supplies were to be taken on at the port of Buin on Bougainville Island and landed at Kaminpo on Guadalcanal Island, one submarine making this trip each day, following a route lying to the southwest of the New Georgia group. When destroyer transport was being used simultaneously, routes and areas of operation were to be fixed in order to avoid congestion. In the event of serious congestion, submarine transport would be canceled. In order to avoid confusion with midget submarine units, all movements were to be carried out south of the bearing 320° from Savo Island. Supplies were to be unloaded mainly in the dark hours after sunset.

During the three months from November, 1942, to early February, 1943, when Guadalcanal Island was finally evacuated, this transport scheme was carried out in the face of heavy losses. Eleven submarines were used early in December, 1942, and a submarine supply line was instituted to Buna in New Guinea for the same reasons as at Guadalcanal.

By January, 1943, there were about twenty submarines engaged on supply duties, including most of the latest types. However, the withdrawal from Guadalcanal was completed on February 7, and after the end of January only two boats in the New Guinea area were still engaged on these duties.

As time passed, progress was made in the method of transport. At first the packages were passed by hand from the inside of the submarine and transferred to motorboats. Then the rice was packed in rubber bags secured to the upper deck, but they got soaked with water, so from January on drums were used instead.

If it was difficult to surface at the appointed landing point, the drums were released and rose to the surface while the submarine remained submerged.

After the middle of January, freight "tubes" were adopted at Guadalcanal and the disembarkation point was fixed in the vicinity of Cape Esperance. A freight "tube" resembled a motor landing craft fitted with a deck; two torpedoes were used for motive power, producing a speed of three knots. Its radius of action was about four thousand yards and it could carry about two tons of supplies. It was piloted by one man who embarked prior to launching, and could be released from a submerged submarine.

There was one other method used in supplying Guadalcanal. This was a tankerlike submarine which was towed and which submerged with the towing submarine. This craft could carry fifty tons of goods but in practice it was very little used.

In early 1943 the island was still being supplied by one submarine a day, but as enemy strength gradually improved our successes correspondingly diminished. However, there was no alternative and these methods of supply continued until the end of the campaign.

Submarine I-1, under a new captain, Lieutenant Commander Sakamoto, left Rabaul on January 26 in preparation for a night supply run to Guadalcanal three days later. At this period supplies were being delivered every two days: one submarine was able to provide the land force of thirty thousand men with two days' supplies. The round trip took four days. From Bougainville on, the voyage was made submerged both by day and by night, only surfacing for about four hours to charge the batteries. The landing point was Kaminpo.

The normal practice was for the submarine to enter the anchorage at dusk with conning tower awash and only proceed inside the reef after a careful inspection. On this occasion I-1 was proceeding as usual and had just raised her periscope at the entrance when she was attacked from astern by an American torpedo boat firing machine guns and torpedoes from a range of about two thousand yards.

Sakamoto at once abandoned the idea of entering the reef, and without waiting to lower the periscope altered course, and gave the order "ninety feet," in a desperate effort to escape. He was too late, and depth charges exploded almost immediately overhead. The inside of the boat was suddenly pitch dark and the concussion was terrific. The main switch on the switchboard went flying and all the motors stopped. Neither the rudders nor pumps would work. The high-pressure air pipes were broken, the batteries were out of action, and confusion reigned in the control room. The boat, with a bow-down angle of forty-five degrees, was plunging to the bottom out of control. Every loose piece of equipment and cargo went tumbling forward as the downward plunge continued. Sakamoto ordered "full astern" on the main motors and the main ballast tanks to be blown. The safe diving depth for I-1 was one hundred and ninety feet, but the depth gauge was hopelessly inaccurate after the depth-charging and was registering four hundred and fifty feet. Suddenly, the man at the after hydroplanes, who was bracing himself for the moment when the boat would cave in owing to excessive water pressure, reported that the needle of the depth gauge was stationary. Then the boat began to rise. Almost simultaneously came the report, "Water coming into the torpedo compartment." All the provisions had slid to the forward part of the submarine, which was becoming increasingly heavy.

Then she broke surface. She went down again but was so heavy forward that it was impossible to proceed submerged. Then the boat appeared to come to rest on the bottom with her bow down at a very steep angle.

The time had come to take the final step. With a struggle the boat was brought to the surface and fire opened on the destroyers and torpedo boats. After only four or five rounds had been fired, enemy machine-gun fire swept the submarine's bridge and completely wiped out everyone except the navigator, who came rushing down the ladder into the control room shouting, "Swords— swords!" This was the first news of the situation on deck. The first lieutenant dashed up to the bridge, sword in hand, and found the gun's crew all killed and no trace of the captain. He immediately summoned the reserve-gun crew and, peering through the gathering darkness, discerned an enemy torpedo boat almost alongside—aft on the port side—why wasn't she firing?

The submarine had left Rabaul with a defective port engine and could only make twelve knots using the starboard engine alone. Consequently the steering was difficult, and at this juncture she suddenly swung round to port, close to the enemy boat. The navigator, who was an expert in swordsmanship, tried to leap aboard the enemy torpedo boat, sword in hand, but the rail being high, he was left hanging on the rail in mid-air by one hand and was unable to pull himself aboard. Then the craft swung apart again.

Once more the enemy opened fire. There seemed to be three or four enemy ships. Soon the petrol in the motor landing craft, which was carried on the after part of the submarine, caught fire. In this glare, as if from a gigantic torch, the attacking ships could probably see the submarine quite plainly, but she could see nothing of them. Meanwhile the enemy switched on his searchlights and two of the submarine chasers opened fire with their 5-cm. guns. The boat was also being fired on by what seemed to be 20-mm. machine guns. There seemed to be two torpedo boats but it was difficult to see clearly. I-1 was still firing but the enemy came round astern and the submarine's gun could not train in that direction. She had removed one gun in order to carry the motor landing craft, so she was at a serious disadvantage. The submarine was firing at the torpedo boat astern with tracer machine gun and rifle, but not getting many hits. On the other hand the submarine, which was well lit up, was being repeatedly hit, particularly in the conning tower, which was holed again and again by the enemy's 5-cm. guns. The steering gear broke down so that hand steering was necessary: the boat was completely out of control.

The torpedo boat fired three torpedoes; fortunately all three missed. While the absorbed first lieutenant was roaring out orders, the submarine's 14-cm. gun scored a hit on the enemy submarine chaser and sank her amid cries of exultation from the submarine's crew. Now one of the enemy torpedo boats launched a sudden attack from the starboard side and the submarine countered with rifle fire. The enemy's fire seemed to weaken —perhaps she had exhausted her ammunition. She came on, and with a crash rammed with the submarine, got free, and made off.

I-1 was on the point of sinking, having fought under extreme difficulty for an hour and a half. Her tanks were badly holed. The first lieutenant decided to run her aground and accordingly turned her head toward the shore. At the very instant the boat grounded, the stern sank, leaving the bow sticking up out of the water, and she settled on the bottom with a big list to port.* The survivors immediately abandoned ship and landed, but those inside the boat failed to escape owing to the sudden inrush of water; over thirty dead were left behind. The remaining fifty assembled on shore, their only weapons two swords and three rifles.

The fact that submarine I-1 kept afloat for so long after being badly holed was remarkable. It was due to the continued operation of the low-pressure discharge pump, a pump which in the ordinary course of events was only used for periods of fifteen minutes, otherwise it would soon run "hot."

When the sinking of the submarine appeared imminent, preparations were made to destroy secret books, but only a few were actually destroyed. If they had been burned ashore, the rising smoke would have attracted enemy aircraft, so they were torn into shreds and buried in the sand. However there was a grave risk that the remainder, left in the submarine, might fall into the hands of the enemy and orders were issued to secure their effective destruction. Eventually three men under an officer waded into the sea under cover of darkness and

---

* I-1 was attacked at 21:05 by two corvettes, *Kiwi* and *Moa*. *Kiwi* rammed I-1 three times and fired her guns till they were too hot to operate. Then *Moa* continued the battle and drove I-1 aground.

sank the protruding parts of the submarine by explosive charges and were afterward withdrawn by destroyer. Nevertheless another submarine was ordered to complete the destruction of I-1 to insure that the secret papers should not be recovered by the enemy. Our own aircraft, too, were ordered to complete the destruction of the boat, but they were unable to detect the submerged remains.*

---

* In spite of these precautions, the U. S. Navy actually recovered a considerable haul of documents from the sunken remains of I-1.

10

TRANSPORT IN

THE FACE OF

ENEMY CONTROL

OF THE SEA

AND AIR

Submarine I-177 under the command of Lieutenant Commander Z. Orita surfaced at the prescribed time and place on September 4, 1943, en route with supplies to Lae. The position there was critical and it looked as if Lae would have to be abandoned after the transfer of I-177's cargo.

According to reports received prior to arrival, a corner of the town was already lost, buildings were on fire, and there was every reason for thinking that the last days were at hand. At last two lighters arrived, the cargo was transferred from the submarine and eighteen men embarked whose condition was so serious as to make it impossible for them to accompany the withdrawal. While this was being done, the submarine was fired on from the shore. Embarkation was hurriedly completed and 1-177 made off, but after she had been under way for five minutes, the lookout reported, "Torpedo boats to starboard." The submarine at once dived to avoid them but when she surfaced again five minutes later, two torpedo boats were again sighted to starboard and I-177 once more submerged. The hydrophones then indicated the presence of five destroyers, and indeed the submarine was surrounded.

There was no question of endangering the lives of the casualties by going into action, so I-177 slipped away quietly and escaped pursuit.

The next objective was Finschhafen, but there I-177 failed—U. S. aircraft were too active. For the third and subsequent attempts, Sio, between Lae and Madang, was used instead of Lae for transferring supplies. It was vital to keep this change of plan very secret. The operation was planned to avoid the period of a week on either side of full moon; the actual transfer was usually carried out about an hour after sunset, and three to five submarines were continually employed on the job. Their carrying capacity was forty to fifty tons inside the boat and twenty to thirty tons on deck. The usual procedure was for a submarine to leave Rabaul on the first day and proceed on the surface, hugging the north coast of New Britain. On the second day it was necessary to proceed submerged in daylight because of the risk of enemy air attacks. The submarine could surface only at night and early dawn to charge the batteries. Three hours before sunset on the third day the boat would then prepare for landing her stores. Arrival at the transfer point was timed for sunset, when the submarine would make known her presence to the troops ashore by raising her periscope and signaling through it with a light. An answering signal would then come from shore.

About half an hour after sunset the boat would surface, await the arrival of the lighter, and transfer both cargo and personnel. It was usually a matter of twenty minutes before the task was completed and the submarine was able to submerge. Woe betide the boat if an aircraft or patrol craft arrived during that time. Unloading was carried out with everyone working at full capacity while the best possible lookouts were alert to spot signs of the enemy. The operation over, the submarine would make off at high speed on the surface until clear of the area, and then proceed submerged and later on the surface as for the outward journey, returning to Rabaul on the seventh day.

These operations did not continue at this tempo for long. After October 20, 1943, the U. S. air attacks on Rabaul increased in intensity, and day raids became a regular routine with the air-raid alarms sounding daily at 10 A.M. At this our naval fighters standing by on the

Eastern Airfield would go up to meet the marauders while the submarines would prepare to submerge, and the cruisers and destroyers weighed anchor in preparation for antiaircraft action. When formations of B-17s, B-25s, and P-38s appeared over Rabaul, the submarines would hasten to submerge at their moorings. One hundred and twenty feet of water provided a very good natural protection! Even so, a bomb dropped nearby would produce uncomfortable reverberations and rocking motions.

Eventually departure for Sio was made before the daily bombing raid and the return to harbor was usually timed for the afternoons. Listening to the results of the daily attacks on Rabaul given by the Imperial H.Q. broadcasts was not very enlightening, but the numbers of fighters able to put up some opposition to the raids and the ships in harbor grew less day by day. At the end of November the American forces occupied a corner of Bougainville, and Rabaul became completely within range of enemy fighters. Although ultimate victory was preached to our soldiers, there was no hiding that defeat in the forward battle area was already a fact.

On November 25, having completed the transport run to Sio and returned to Rabaul, we were taking a hurried nap in the barracks when we were awakened by the alarm and were summoned to H.Q. That night three destroyers with units on board who were withdrawing from Bougainville Island to Rabaul were surrounded by the enemy and sunk ninety miles to the west of Cape St. George. Orders were therefore received to proceed forthwith to their rescue. We proceeded at full speed to the scene of action without waiting for daybreak, taking avoiding action to escape the attentions of patrol craft and planes. When we eventually surfaced, we found a huge area covered with castaways—in fact, we had come to the surface right in the middle of them. Keeping a careful lookout for the approach of hostile aircraft, rescue of the survivors began. With the approach of sunset rescue operations grew bolder. Life buoys were thrown and the crew leaped overboard to help bring in the wounded. By the time it was dark there were no survivors left in sight, and in all two hundred and twenty-seven people had been taken on board, making it practically impossible for anyone to move inside the submarine. Just as we set off for home, two bombs were dropped by radar-equipped enemy planes. The boat rapidly submerged. The crush down below was appalling. The surgeon and sick-berth attendants were hard at work tending the wounded. The tropical heat and smell of oil made conditions unbearable. We couldn't remain submerged for long for fear of the effects of carbon dioxide, and after two hours surfaced and made for Rabaul, where we arrived at 8 A.M. on the following day, November 26. Having disembarked survivors, we left again on a second rescue operation.

By December the Allied armies had landed on the western end of New Britain Island and our route to Sio was cut off. Enemy torpedo craft, fast and difficult to locate, were very active. Our torpedoes were of no avail against them, but their depth charges were deadly. On January 1, 1944, while we were in the midst of Distant Emperor Worship, Rabaul received a heavy air raid. As usual, we submerged and lay on the bottom. In Rabaul harbor, instead of over two hundred ships, as when submarine RO-101 first arrived, there was only an odd submarine or so at anchor, and as these had to submerge on the occasion of an air raid, there wasn't a single ship to be seen.

On January 2 we were summoned to H.Q., where we learned that the H.Q. of the 18th Army and the 18th Naval Base Force were surrounded; operations to relieve them were planned. To use the escape route by land through the jungle to Madang would involve a two months' campaign. This was turned down and it was decided to effect the evacuation by sea in submarines. We were to proceed to the rescue with all dispatch.

Entreaties for our success were received from both the naval and army commanders as we set out for Sio on the evening of January 3. As usual, it was the intention to arrive at the embarkation point about half an hour after sunset, but an unexpectedly strong current was encountered. We were still five miles short at the appointed hour, but by pressing on at full speed on the surface we arrived only twenty minutes late. The two motor landing craft with the H.Q. Staff on board were just coming alongside when a shout of, "Two enemy torpedo boats," came from the lookout. Hurriedly securing the gear on the upper deck and telling the landing craft that we would come again tomorrow, we dived and put out to sea. The torpedo boats were milling round overhead and after thirty minutes came the sound of the explosion of two depth charges which the torpedo boats dropped as a parting gesture before withdrawing. The submarine passed that night at a point thirty miles from Sio. The next morning we arrived at the rendezvous as before and received the signal from shore, but again a torpedo boat appeared and the operation was postponed for yet another day. This time, however, the submarine spent the night in the vicinity, resolving to surface as soon as the torpedo boat had departed. The enemy, however, had marked the diving position and fired four depth charges. Fortunately the submarine suffered no damage as she was deep and the charges were small.

On January 8 it was decided to force the operation through even though it involved action with the torpedo boat and therefore we arrived once more at the embarkation point and signaled, "We're O.K. Prepare to embark." The boat surfaced dead on time and the landing craft came alongside. The personnel embarked and went below and we had just begun to take the equipment on board when the lookout reported, "Torpedo boats!" They appeared to be just on the horizon—that meant action in two or three minutes, so the submarine dived rapidly. At that instant came the thud of hits made by several shells, perhaps on the landing craft, and the sound of rapid fire. The boat dived to one hundred and eighty feet and set course for Madang. There was no pursuit. Inside the submarine the crew reverted from action stations to normal three-watch stations. We were able to relax and welcome the naval and army commanders, who seemed more than grateful for their rescue.

After dark the boat surfaced and made good speed under the friendly cover of a thunderstorm, submerging again at dawn to arrive off the Madang harbor entrance about sunset, only to find a raid by P-38s in progress. After the raid was over, we surfaced and landed our passengers. The operation was over, successfully.

It had been nearly a year since I-177 had left home waters, and she was badly in need of a refit. Furthermore, as Rabaul was no longer a safe anchorage, she left that place of many memories on January 10, 1944, for Truk in the Carolines. Many submarines had operated from Rabaul, and of them no less than eight had failed to return.

11

THE DESPERATE

STRUGGLE

OF I-176

At the beginning of the war Lieutenant Aragi was with me as navigator in I-24 and subsequently became torpedo officer of submarine I-176, which was engaged in transport to the Lae area. The following is the story of his experiences:

"On March 19, 1943, submarine I-176, assigned to transport duties in the Lae area, surfaced under cover of dusk in position about four hundred meters west of the prearranged disembarkation point off the Lae coast.

"The captain was Commander Tanabe, who was famous throughout the Navy for his sinking of the U. S. carrier *Yorktown* at the battle of Midway. The crew had been specially picked after the boat was fitted out in May, 1942. Furthermore, I-176 had successfully carried out the first submarine transport operation to Guadalcanal, and on October 20, 1942, had sunk a *Texas*-class battleship in the same area*; she also further distinguished herself in subsequent transport operations to the Guadalcanal area.

"The shore base authorities, who were impatiently waiting for the submarine, sent out the landing craft without waiting for the recognition signal and these were now approaching. The submarine's crew were ready at their stations awaiting the order to commence unloading. Since the beginning of these Guadalcanal transport operations most of the submarines in the area had been taken off their normal duties and were now quite *au fait* with the problems of transporting personnel, ammunition, and supplies. The crews, too, were fully aware of the serious situation with which we were faced. When we had to tell our subordinates about these somewhat unwelcome duties, we had been rather doubt-

---

* The U. S. cruiser *Chester* was torpedoed by I-176 on October 20, halfway between Espiritu Santo and San Cristobal. She was damaged in No. 1 engine room but was able to proceed to Norfolk for repairs, and rejoined the Pacific fleet in time for the Gilberts operation.

ful of their reactions. However, it seemed that they fully appreciated the war situation and were overcoming their natural feelings by throwing themselves heart and soul into their new duties, despite the frequent bad news about sister ships. In I-176 there was no such word as 'can't'—.

"At length the landing craft were secured alongside, and at an order from the captain the work of transporting the stores commenced. The crew were specially organized for the task and all went like clockwork. To those ashore the bags of rice brought by I-176 were their means of subsistence, and they regarded us as a god of rescue.

"Darkness was setting in and the work half completed when several rockets were fired from the shore signal station; these were followed by the sound of continuous machine-gun fire. The captain gave the order to dive, and I dashed down the conning tower. But we were not in time to escape an attack by three medium bombers, and just as my feet touched the control-room deck there was the sound of bombs and machine-gun bullets. I felt a concussion which seemed to send the boat lunging upward, and she started to heel over to port. I tottered over to support myself against the control-room bulkhead, and for a moment all the breath was knocked out of my body. The next thing I heard was the order, 'Blow port main ballast.' The boat shuddered and remained heeled over; then she slowly righted herself. Amid all the confusion of the falling bombs and machine-gun fire, the crew came crowding into the boat. The depth gauge was moving very slowly. The machine-gun bullets were spraying the conning tower as if in pursuit of the escaping crew. One bullet hit the quartermaster at the wheel in the back of the head, and he died in a sitting posture without a word. Amid all the confusion in the stern of the boat there were some who were silent—when I tried to speak to them I realized they were dying.

"Someone shouted, 'She's leaking.' An inspection revealed water coming in through the middle of the conning-tower deck on the port side—then the W/T cabin was also reported to be leaking. The order was given: 'Shut water-tight doors.' Tucking up the trousers worn over their tropical clothing, the crew tried to close the doors by hand, but the pressure of the water only increased.

"Water was already coming through the upper deck as far as the control room. When I looked round for the captain he was sitting abaft the after periscope, murmuring, 'I've had it, Number One,' in a labored voice; his breathing appeared to be difficult.

"Finally, when the yeoman of signals shut the hatch, we could hear the sound of the water pouring over the bridge deck, for the boat had dived without opening the main vents. While this was happening the landing craft had scattered in all directions, and, according to their observations, the splashes and flashes caused by the bombs and machine guns during the enemy attack had for an instant enveloped the whole submarine, particularly the bomb which hit the after part, throwing up a column of flame. Then the boat seemed to list further and further to port, going down all the time, and they thought that she had sunk. Later a signal was intercepted

The author, Lieutenant Commander Hashimoto, at the periscope of I-58.

Submarine I-58, the author's command—and one of the few Japanese submarines to survive the war.

Above: I-10 leaves Penang on an Indian Ocean patrol. *Below:* I-10 on patrol.

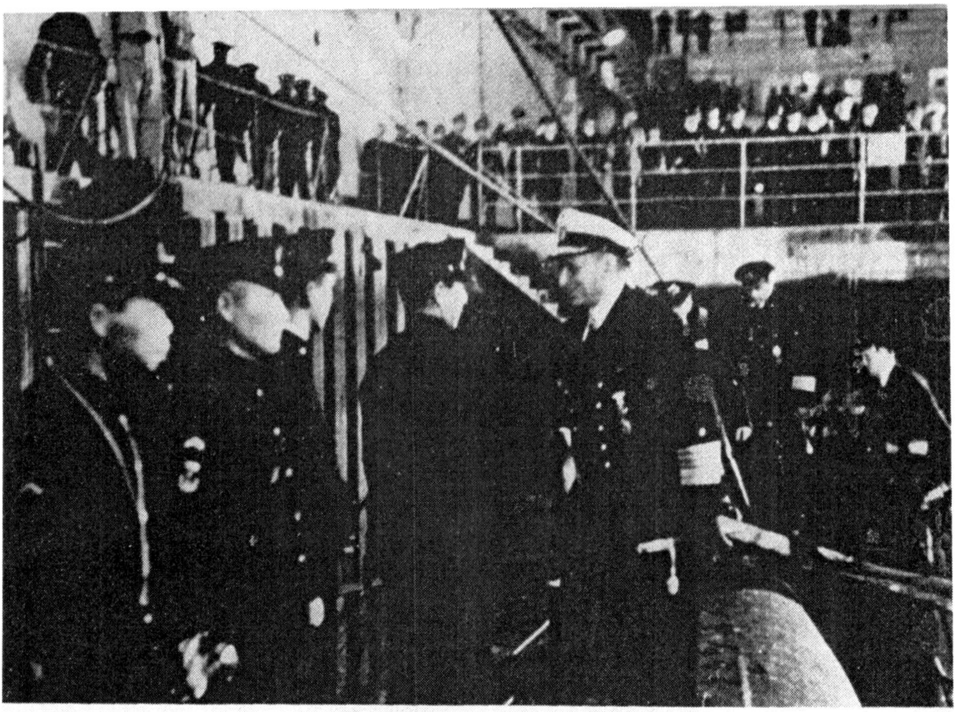

Admiral Kranke of the German Navy welcomes the captain and crew of I-8 at Brest.

I-368 leaves port for operations at Iwo Jima, carrying her complement of Kaitens—human torpedoes—on deck.

A Kaiten on its mounting.

Ceremonial graduation of the Kaiten crews at the special training base.

reporting the sinking of a destroyer, and so it seemed that the enemy thought they had finished off the job. It was nothing more than a piece of good fortune that they did not return to the attack.

"The damage we had suffered was already formidable. A signalman and the quartermaster were dead, the captain and another signalman severely injured, and the pressure hull was pierced. There were holes five centimeters in diameter on the port side of both the conning tower and W/T cabin. Pipes were fractured in many places in the low-pressure air lines, the trimming tanks were flooded, and the main ballast tank and fuel tank were holed in many places.

"This damage was confirmed by more thorough investigation. So, having got all the crew inside the boat, we explained the dangerous situation. The fate of I-176 hung in the balance.

"By blowing the port main tank continuously we eventually got the list off the boat and stopped her sinking, but this used up a large quantity of high-pressure air and the chances were that we would not be able to blow the boat up further. In any case, the air from the main tanks and the air lines was rapidly escaping and the boat was getting heavy. The conning tower was still leaking. Water was streaming in through the periscope glands and the damage-control party was desperately trying to plug the holes with rags, or anything that came to hand, while others were cutting wooden plugs from spars.

"The receivers in the W/T cabin, which were secured with rivets, were disconnected, as the damaged portion of the cabinet was behind the receivers, and the work was further delayed by having to collect together the spare parts from the store. With the captain mortally wounded, the command of the boat devolved on me as the first lieutenant. Thus the fate of the boat was in my hands.

"I had to decide whether to remain submerged or surface, but the sight of the water gushing in made me realize at once that to continue submerged would merely lead to our complete destruction.

"Still, I didn't think we could surface properly with the small amount of high-pressure air remaining. Even if we managed to surface for a short while, there was the risk of a further enemy attack. This would amount to handing the boat to the enemy on a plate. I racked my brains to find a solution, and then almost intuitively I said, 'Captain! We'll run ourselves aground and carry out repairs.' The captain nodded silently in assent. This was undoubtedly the wisest course of action. As we would be grounding on the coast at deep draught, we should be able to get off without too much difficulty, in spite of the abnormal tide fluctuation. Having grounded, we could devote all our resources to investigating and repairing the damage and carry out the work in secret in the shade of the jungle trees away from the prying eyes of the enemy. Even though we could carry out emergency repairs on the surface, we should be continually worrying about the boat's stability, and, moreover, only a limited amount of work would be possible if we were not to be late for submerging the following day. Then, again, if we grounded in surface trim, we probably wouldn't be able to refloat owing to the big rise and fall in tide, and might remain permanently exposed on the Lae coast.

"Since the enemy attack, the actions of the crew had been entirely automatic or instinctive, but the fact that they didn't lose control must either be attributed to the unseen guidance of the gods or to a manifestation of our latent powers of endurance in emergency.

"Wading through the sea water, I went to look through the periscope; I could see only a succession of black spots, the reflection of land, sea, or air—it was impossible to know which.

"After some intense concentration I made out a river entrance. The sea bottom in the South Seas is studded with coral reefs, and one cannot rely on charts. This had been brought out clearly by my experiences on a reconnaissance of Buna when we got lost in a maze of reefs and had great difficulty in getting out. There was nothing to do but to make straight for this river entrance if we were to run ourselves aground.

"I ordered 'Full speed astern' and I-176 backed slowly and erratically toward the river mouth. The depth-gauge needle slowly moved from twenty-four to twenty-seven. I was conscious that all eyes were on the needle shining dimly in the light on the depth-gauge panel, the only light burning in the dark control room. Then the needle started to move back slightly—the crisis was past as we were reaching shallow water. The water stopped coming through the holes—'We've stopped leaking, everything's all right,'—my voice quivered with joy.

"The shadow of land loomed large in the periscope —'slow astern'—'stop'—'full astern' were ordered in quick succession as the boat touched the ground with a slight shudder. She came to a stop at only a small angle. Relief showed on the faces of those in the control room. The sound of the repeat call, 'both engines stopped,' echoed through the ship and was then silent. Amid the strange quiet we had returned to the land.

"The tension slackened but after a brief pause we began to think of the hazards of our present position and the future difficulties to be overcome. Time was the all-important factor. At this moment the tide was just on the ebb. We must go on deck, carry out essential repairs and get off by high tide in time to carry out our next assignment. Whatever the depth-gauge needle was showing, the bridge should be above water. We tried easing the hatch handle. No water came through. Having fully opened the hatch, I went on deck and searched in all directions with binoculars, but all was quiet and there was nothing in sight. Only the bows and the bridge deck were above water. I posted bridge lookouts and pulled out and lit a cigarette with a shaking hand. Strangely enough the sight of me smoking had the effect of calming the people around me—at least that is what I was told afterward. The boat then had to be got further out of the water so that repair work might begin. I ordered, 'Blow main ballast tanks,' and soon the upper deck and the bulges of the main tanks were visible. I stopped blowing and shut the Kingston valves. Throughout the whole of the upper deck came the hissing sound of escaping air. The consumption of high-pressure air had been heavy and we had used up the greater part of the supply in the air bottles.

"The repair party standing by in the control room was soon on the upper deck, investigating the damage and effecting repairs. We started the air compressor. The repair party found many of the holes by playing the air jets on the inside of the hull, while others passed their hands over the deck from the outside, where they found that of necessity they had to tear up the deck planking to facilitate their search. At this juncture the chief engineer came on the bridge and said that there would be difficulty in returning to Rabaul in view of the state of damage and what about transferring ashore? In a submarine a big list has a great psychological effect and I knew that the crew felt that 'they'd had it' when the boat took up a big list after the bombing attack. I explained the situation to the chief engineer and told him, 'The boat has been badly damaged but this does not mean that she is out of action. I am confident that we can get back to Rabaul after effecting emergency repairs. I am determined to stick it out to the end even though we should be attacked by the enemy.' The sentiments that I conveyed to him in these words had the effect of strengthening my own resolve.

"Having a spare moment, I went to see the captain in his cabin. His face was dead white owing to loss of blood and he was not fully conscious. 'If I'm going to die like this it would have been better for the bullet to have finished me off,' he said. I told him that no completion of repairs I hoped to get off at high tide and make our escape before dawn, after making a trial dive. His reaction to this was that it would be better to spend the whole of the next day lying on the bottom in order to confirm that the boat was really seaworthy.

"While I had the feeling that we all wanted to get back as soon as possible, I thought over the captain's advice and came round to the idea that it would be better to spend a day on the bottom, confirm the boat's seaworthiness, and conserve the energies of the crew.

"Through the crew's efforts, the holes were being plugged one by one. Only simple remedies in the shape of cloth patches and wooden wedges were being used, but these would be enough to make the boat fit for diving. But the holes were very numerous. While there were some up to twenty-six centimeters wide, for which patches could be prepared, the most numerous were only about five centimeters in diameter, and it took a long time to make wooden plugs for these. The first supply of plugs the men had prepared soon ran out. When we examined the bomb damage on deck a ten-centimeter hole was found in the port main tank but that was all. The after-deck had in fact been stacked with rice containers and it seemed that the enemy bomb had exploded over the top of them.

"The landing craft which had been searching for us at last sighted the submarine and approached our side. They were very surprised to see the submarine perched up on the beach for they were sure we had been sunk. We asked them to come and take over the ammunition, medical stores, and provisions still remaining on board, also the two wounded. I told the captain, 'We have no facilities for looking after you on board and as the journey to Rabaul will be dangerous I would like to put you ashore,' but he emphatically refused. The bodies of the two dead, the wounded, and some of the ammunition were transferred to the landing craft which then made off— watched in silence by the crew.

"At length, four more landing craft appeared and took off the remainder of the arms, ammunition, and provisions. Our assignment was thus completed. The officer in charge of the landing craft shook me by the hand and wished us a safe passage to Rabaul. At last the tide was on the flood, and by midnight the hull which had been exposed to show the mouths of the torpedo tubes, was down in the water to water-line paint mark.

"We put air through the low-pressure system to see if any holes were left and generally tested the results of our emergency repair work, practically all of which was completed by high tide. Air bottles were topped up and batteries charged and the boat was back to normal.

"The time had come for trying to get off. I put the motors full astern but she didn't budge. It seemed as if the keel was fairly well buried in the sand.

"I tried surging the crew from one side of the boat to the other, at the same time running the motors full astern, sending the swirl of the propellers on to the boat's bottom, which gradually set up a rolling motion and loosened her. I changed to main engines, went full astern, and at length she came off. The crew were overcome with joy and were positively shouting with approval, rushing up on the bridge, and offering their congratulations.

"We dived at dawn but the dive proved to be full of

anxiety, contrary to our earlier feeling that everything would be plain sailing. We came to rest on the bottom at one hundred and twenty feet. The sea bottom was apparently undulating, for there was a fifteen-degree angle on the boat. There were no leaks through the recently repaired holes; I had a man posted in each compartment to keep a lookout for water. Those not on watch got their heads down and took a well-earned sleep.

"I drifted round the boat in tired fashion, inspecting each compartment, and spotted that the water gauge of one of the trimming tanks was steadily rising. There was undoubtedly a hole somewhere but it couldn't be found, and it would have to be left until we got back to Rabaul when the base repair staff would be able to make a detailed inspection.

"The bullet holes were below the water line and one couldn't get at them. Nevertheless this one bullet hole was to give rise to a dangerous situation the following day, though at the time this didn't seem likely. I myself was extremely tired and I threw myself down on my bed and sank into a deep sleep. When I eventually woke and looked at my watch it was nearly sunset.

"We had spent a whole day on the bottom without any trouble with leaks through the patched-up holes, but when we surfaced I had a feeling that the hull was pretty heavy. Perhaps there had been a leak from the pipes which we hadn't noticed while asleep. A look through the periscope confirmed that it was growing dark. I ordered the crew to diving stations and made out of the bay at eighteen knots.

"The night of the 20th passed without incident and

we dived again at dawn on the 21st. If this dive period passed over safely, there would remain only the night passage to the vicinity of Rabaul. We got rather worried as the water in the holed trimming tank was gradually increasing, and we were going along with the discharge pump running incessantly.

"At about noon the tank we were using for adjusting buoyancy ran dry. What was to be done? If we surfaced, it was quite clear that we would be spotted by the enemy patrol aircraft. One method was to transfer the oil fuel in the ballast tank to the main tank, but there was a fear that the oil would leak from the holes in the main tank. We could also jettison the torpedoes from the tubes and any other heavy gear, but I didn't want to do this except as a last resort.

"As a temporary measure we blew air to the midships starboard main ballast tank and then adjusted the trim by admitting water to the trimming tank. The blowing was strictly controlled in order to prevent a leakage of air which would give our position away. Owing to the blowing of the starboard ballast tank, the boat had a list of three degrees to port, but this was not enough to cause any accident. This procedure was repeated two or three times during the afternoon and we held on till sunset and surfaced at dark. It was a clear starlit night and the sea was calm.

"It was the kind of night we had long been waiting for and the engines were running smoothly. Despite the high speed we maintained (eighteen knots), we made no smoke, and taken all in all our spirits were high, but there was no question of relaxing. It must have been when we were passing halfway along the coast of New Britain, keeping a strict lookout with the crew at diving stations, that there was a sudden shout, 'Enemy aircraft.' On reducing speed and looking in the direction indicated by the lookout, sure enough there was an enemy flying boat. Soon there came a hail of machine-gun bullets. I ordered, 'Open fire with antiaircraft armament!' and we followed the enemy plane round with machine-gun fire from our 13-mm. double-barreled machine gun.

"Having lost the initiative, it would have been fatal for the boat to dive right under the eyes of the enemy. It was better to fight! The enemy passed over from starboard and disappeared and I gave the order to cease fire. We made a big alteration of course and continued on our way.

"But it seemed that the enemy had radar and he came up again, this time from astern. Then almost immediately a bomb exploded right in our wake. The nearer the enemy came, the greater the danger, and we kept up continuous machine-gun fire. We could see through binoculars that we had hit the wing of the enemy—our upper deck was covered with expended cartridge cases. The engine-room personnel tried to bring rifles on to the bridge, asking to have a crack at the enemy. I told them that rifles were no good, and put them on to helping the ammunition supply. The enemy bullets fell all around us but fortunately caused no damage. Soon he appeared to get disheartened and made off.

"Perhaps he would come again—and so he did!

"This time it was a little different. He fired completely at random and then made off for good without coming close. We had not been able to shoot down the enemy plane but we had put up a good defense, which put the crew in very high spirits—there was a feeling of security in that we were getting close to our base and the whole atmosphere in the boat brightened up. At last dawn came, and a lovely dawn it was, the like of which we hadn't seen for a long time.

"We entered Rabaul harbor during the forenoon of the 22nd and our arduous operational transport duty was over."

"It was the time of the battle of Lae. Submarine I-176 had been refitted in home waters and the enemy aircraft's machine-gun damage had been made good. She had returned to Rabaul for the second time with a new captain —Lieutenant Commander K. Yamaguchi—and had another narrow escape while on her return journey from Lae.

"She was proceeding on the surface by night when suddenly a star shell burst overhead. The captain ordered, 'Crash-dive,' and submerged, turning the while. At the point when the upper deck was just under water, we felt something heavy hit the bridge. There was no time to ascertain what it was and we went down to forty-five feet—just at that moment there was the sound of something bursting overhead, but it was rather a small explosion to be caused by a bomb. Feeling a little anxious, we went down further and came to rest at ninety feet. As the boat was rather heavy, there was no stopping in the middle of a crash dive. We remained submerged for a short time and surfaced at daylight, as we could expect to be within our own patrol area. To our surprise we found the forward bulkhead of the bridge stove in, a long cylindrical object lodged in the cavity, and the magnetic compass fallen over on its side. A closer inspection revealed the words 'depth charge' written in English on the casing. The bridge deck was covered all over with a kind of yellow mudlike substance. This was the bursting charge of the depth charge.

"This depth charge dropped by the enemy aircraft had missed the diving submarine, hit the water, bounded up against the bridge, and broken up. The bursting charge had been soaked by the salt water, and when the submarine was down to forty-five feet the fuse had gone off according to its setting, but had failed to ignite the bursting charge. It was a tremendous stroke of luck. We delivered the depth charge to the base authorities."

12

THE AIR

ATTACK

ON THE

TRUK BASE

In January, 1944, I was in command of submarine RO-
44 and was ordered to proceed to the eastern Solomons
area with the aim of cutting the enemy's rear supply
lines. At this period, since many of our submarines had
failed to return from such operations, special precautions

were very necessary, especially in selecting the routes to be followed. Journeys were limited to areas which were expected to be free of enemy submarines and patrol air-craft. If it became necessary to pass through areas within the radius of action of enemy search aircraft, subma-rines had to proceed submerged both by day and by night. After crossing the equator, the heat made condi-tions in the boats very trying though an air-conditioning plant was fitted to keep the temperature down to reason-able limits.

When we got near Truk we could see the reflection of sheets of flame in the night sky. There were sounds of frequent explosions, and we soon realized that the situa-tion was hopeless. We arrived off the reef before dawn. There was no sighting the enemy. We waited four days, patrolling off Truk, surfaced by night and submerged during daylight. By then there was little left of our month's supply of provisions. Eventually we received or-ders to enter Truk harbor. Finding a suitable route was tricky, for it was difficult to see a safe passage through the remains of our sunken ships. However, we got in with-out mishap. The sight of capsized and sunken ships, their masts sticking forlornly out of the water, was most des-olate. We anchored off the submarine base. The depot ship had sunk at her moorings and all her valuable submarine supplies had gone down with her.

I went ashore to make my report at H.Q. I found the staff wondering whether we had been sunk, as no signals had been received. RO-39 had signaled from a point off Wotje, but the message was undecipherable and she was never heard of again.

The tempo of the U. S. western advance after occupying the Marshalls had been fast.

The staggering enemy attack on Truk was a natural corollary to their occupation of the Marshalls. A large enemy force of aircraft carriers had attacked on February 17, 1944. Truk had held an important position as the central base for our operations in the Solomons and Marshalls and was also the Combined Fleet base, until enemy occupation of the Marshalls forced the Combined Fleet to withdraw to Palau.

At the time of the enemy attack, although our air patrols could hardly be termed completely adequate, they were making air searches in areas in which the enemy might be expected. On this particular day only half the normal number of planes had been up, due to a heavy storm, and these had already returned to base. The enemy, however, made his approach during the height of the storm. Without warning a vast number of enemy carrier-borne aircraft suddenly appeared over Truk. The first attack was concentrated on the Takeshima air base. Fighters were sent up in an endeavor to intercept —some among them without any machine-gun ammunition. These aircraft were nearly all shot down and six warships and twenty-six of our transports were sunk. Aircraft losses amounted to one hundred and eighty planes. Enemy battleships appeared outside the reef, and soon our precious oil fuel supplies were alight. They burned for several days, making a splendid illumination of the target for night attacks carried out by U. S. B-17 bombers.

Under these conditions Rabaul ceased to have any

value as an air base, and the air units there were withdrawn; the Solomons were abandoned to the enemy. Thus the outer battle area had to be abandoned and defensive action taken to keep the inner zone secure. In other words, the front changed from Saipan-Guam to Philippines-Okinawa. If these islands, too, were lost to the enemy we would be faced with a direct attack on the Japanese home country.

The submarines at Rabaul were withdrawn after the departure of the air units, and were charged with supplying food to the beleaguered forces on Mille Island in the Marshalls. Four vessels left Truk in the midst of the air attack laden with food and tobacco on the upper deck and 25-mm. machine-gun ammunition down below. Having passed the enemy submarine danger area, the boats proceeded on the surface during daylight hours. Unfortunately the special fittings erected on the deck of our submarine to contain the food supplies began to carry away. Although we reduced speed, the whole lot had been lost by the time the destination was reached. There was therefore nothing to do but to return, carry out repairs, and start again.

Once more we set off, loaded with supplies. On entering the area in the Marshalls controlled by the enemy, we remained submerged, as it was most important not to be sighted if the expedition were not to end in a failure. There was already a fear that the plan was known, for it was suspected that the code held by the unit on Mille Island was being read by the enemy. We were carrying a new code for the unit, but the message announcing our visit had been made in the old code. Having passed Jaluit safely, we altered course for Mille. It was a bright moonlit night. We sighted something like the mast of a ship right ahead on the horizon and immediately crash-dived. Sure enough it was a battleship, with two aircraft carriers astern. It was a heaven-sent opportunity. We increased speed and tried to get nearer. The battleship was already quite close, but as we watched through the periscope the carriers seemed to be dropping astern. Then, suddenly, they altered course away. Perhaps we had been spotted! We surfaced and went in pursuit, but owing to their superior speed they gave us no chance of getting within striking distance. After about another hour we again sighted a ship's mast, dived to periscope depth, and saw six destroyers in line abreast approaching at a fairly high speed. The carrier force we had sighted had been without escorting destroyers. Perhaps these were the escort reforming at high speed. Or were they an antisubmarine sweeping unit? They seemed to be slackening speed and certainly looked to us like an antisubmarine sweeping flotilla. We altered course to avoid attention. Periscope observation confirmed that the unit was in single line abreast, an easy formation for torpedo attack—should we attack? The torpedoes in readiness for the carriers were waiting to be fired, but in fact our sailing orders defined our principal duty as supply and reconnaissance. It was in order to depart from these instructions if the target were a battleship or aircraft carrier, otherwise our main duty had priority; other enemy craft were forbidden targets. This had been agreed with the senior staff officer before we sailed. Thus, regretfully, we had to let the opportunity go. When the enemy ships had passed out of sight we surfaced. We had used a considerable amount of battery power and we therefore recharged at high speed while making to the east for Mille. At daybreak we dived again and arrived off Mille at nightfall on the following day, and proceeded to investigate conditions at the spot proposed for landing supplies. The moon was shining, the visibility was good, and there was no sign of the enemy. It had been arranged to release the food canisters from the upper deck while submerged, but there seemed no need for such precautions. We asked by semaphore if the passage down the channel ahead of us was clear, received an affirmative, and we entered inside the reef. Enemy reconnaissance planes often came over at night, so we lay submerged inside the reef while the food canisters were released. When this was safely over we surfaced and contacted the second-in-command of the shore unit, from whom we received presents and thanks for our trouble. They had been waiting a long time for their mail and food supplies; they were subject to daily air raids and were living in the jungle.

Nothing was known of the conditions in Mejuro, about fifty miles away. The soldiers who came to take over the supplies seemed to want tobacco rather than food. We handed over a case of cigarettes, and in addition we gave them all that was left of our own supply on board. Their appetite for tobacco seemed a bit strange to me, a non-smoker. Nevertheless, we felt very sorry for them, for their situation was not enviable.

We were to go on to investigate the position at Mejuro

and therefore asked the Mille garrison to signal the unit there, using the new code, saying that we were on our way. We left at about 7 P.M. On the day before an enemy plane had dropped some mines just outside the reef. Most of them had fallen on shore and the reef was reported to be all right. The passage out was nevertheless somewhat nerve-wracking. However, we got out safely and set course for Mejuro.

. At 11 P.M. on the 12th we suddenly had the order to crash-dive—a red light had been sighted ahead. Through the periscope the number of lights increased as we got nearer. Suddenly there appeared a whole row of lights like a lantern procession. It seemed undoubtedly an aerodrome. All hands turned in to await the dawn. By 3:30 A.M. it was light enough to see that our supposed aerodrome was a group of enemy naval craft: eight enemy battleships, an aircraft carrier, and some tank landing craft lay inside a reef. The range of the nearest battleship was only five or six hundred yards. Immediately orders were given to stand by to take a periscope photograph. Then we realized that our supply mission would be endangered by such a close approach to the enemy. We could see twin-engined aircraft landing and taking off from the carrier. After observing the enemy for some time, we retreated to a safe distance. Having charged our batteries, it was by then quite dark, and we proceeded on the surface with the idea of reconnoitering the entrance to Mejuro reef. There was a lot of mist and the visibility was bad, but the sea was comparatively calm. We sighted an aircraft with a white light and dived to evade. It appeared, however, to be on its return run and showed no signs of searching for us. When we surfaced again we sighted a black horizontal object, which, through the periscope, appeared to be a destroyer. We altered course sixteen points and waited for dawn. We looked again when it was light and confirmed that the object was in fact a destroyer. Every time we made a good enemy sighting it was with the special binoculars recently supplied. We turned back on to our course, but no land came in sight. We approached another island that seemed to have an airstrip, but there were no signs of any aircraft and we must have been mistaken. Altering course away from this island, we were continuing on our way westward when we heard the sound of propellers of a patrol vessel. There turned out to be two of them. We took evading action and at 6 P.M. on the 13th, after being submerged for twenty hours, no further sounds of propellers were heard.

Having taken a good look round, we surfaced and reported to the C.-in-C. Combined Fleet: "One enemy aircraft carrier, eight battleships, and other major units at anchor inside Mejuro reef. Also aerodrome being used by medium-type aircraft." After charging our batteries we made a more detailed report, giving the exact composition of the enemy force. Our task thus safely accomplished, we returned to Truk at the end of March. On the return passage we sighted a merchant ship, but an inquiry to H.Q. revealed it to be one of our own.

I went ashore to make my official report and was asked why I didn't attack the destroyer. I reported that I had acted in accordance with my sailing orders and that the reconnaissance could not be regarded as complete until the report on Mejuro was safely transmitted. However, I always bitterly regretted not having been able to make an attack. It was surprising to find that all four submarines which had sailed with us had returned to Truk. True, they hadn't all carried out their allotted tasks, but it was a long time since all boats had returned safely from an operation. Some four months later, by the end of the battle of Saipan, the other three captains had all been killed in action and I was the only one left.

I-32 had already left on her second supply trip to Mille, but the supplies never reached their destination and nothing more was ever heard of her. In all probability the American patrols had increased in intensity. We heard after the war that I-32 had been sunk by the U. S. fleet off Mille on March 24. On the 31st two aircraft carrying Admiral Koga, the C.-in-C. Combined Fleet, and his staff left Palau, but they never reached their destination and nothing more was heard of them. All operations were virtually brought to a standstill.

Enemy air attacks on Truk were increasing in intensity and every day the submarines remaining there had to be on the bottom to escape destruction. Even under these conditions, however, the three-watch system was still in operation and those not on watch were allowed ashore. While lying on the bottom, I-169 had a compartment flooded. After the air raid was over she failed to surface. Attempts to lift her were made without success —the raising wires carried away and eventually all hope of rescue was abandoned. Rescue operations in the midst of constant air raids eventually became impossible.

Later the enemy bombed the anchorage where the submarines lay on the bottom. The anchorage was shallow, the depth being only about seventy-five feet. They dropped some bombs directly over the boat I was serving in—RO-44—but although she was shaken violently, there was no flooding. When we surfaced we found the periscopes considerably damaged. Since repairs could not be effected at Truk, we slipped out of harbor one night en route for Japan. We got safely through the area where enemy submarines might be lurking, and after leaving Saipan far away to the east we proceeded at high speed on the surface both by day and by night. On one occasion while I was on the bridge, the lookout reported a friendly aircraft. The plane was approaching on the beam and I, too, was inclined to think it was friendly, but on taking a second look, it was obvious that the plane was making straight for us—it was an enemy! I immediately gave the order to dive. By this time, however, the aircraft was nearly overhead and if we were to be bombed, it would be better to be on the surface than just below it, so the order was countermanded. In the last seconds while we waited for the bombs to drop the enemy seemed to hesitate as if in some doubt as to whether we were friend or foe. Then the bombs fell. There were two splashes, only fifteen to thirty feet astern of us. However there was no damage and we made to dive, as fast as possible. We had hardly got down to the level of the conning-tower deck when the enemy had turned and fired at us with his machine guns. A moment later we were safely under cover of the sea. When we surfaced about an hour later, there were some holes on deck made by machine-gun bullets.

We expected another visit the next day and kept a very good lookout in the direction of the sun. Just as the sun was going down in the late afternoon, the enemy appeared again. We dived and waited for about an hour but nothing transpired.

We arrived at Kure on April 29, and a new captain took over. It was his first command and for a time we went out on exercises together. Eventually RO-44 was sunk by a U. S. destroyer off Eniwetok on June 5, 1944.

13

OPERATIONS

IN THE

NORTH

The mere mention of this area conjures up visions of blinding snowstorms, rough seas, and fog. In the winter particularly, the weather is subject to very sudden changes and a calm sea can suddenly turn extremely rough in hurricane-like conditions. Areas of low pressure are very frequent and there was once a case of a warship capsizing due to the gale and mountainous seas. Even in spring when it becomes a little warmer, there is still incessant fog. Although the shortest route between Japan and the U.S.A. runs through these waters, it never became a main theater of operations for there were few days in the year when ships and aircraft could operate without a natural hindrance of some kind. This applied in a big measure to submarines and other small vessels. If a submarine put on any speed in these high seas, the glass on the bridge would get broken. It was necessary to fit steel baffles to counteract this. The hands of the lookouts, holding binoculars, would freeze, and the icy wind would go right through cold-weather clothing to the very marrow. Even submerged, where there was no wind, it was an existence in a steel tube washed by sea water whose temperature was never far from zero. It was just like being shut up in an ice chest, causing one to shiver despite warm winter clothing, which being very bulky, made it difficult to pass along the narrow passages below deck. Thus life in a submarine in these waters was no sinecure!

In contrast to other warships, submarine crews, both officers and men, left the majority of their personal effects at the base or on board the depot ship, and only took the minimum amount to sea. Therefore when changing station from the warm climate of the southern seas to the cold north, submarines had to put into their home ports to pick up winter clothing, which took up far more room than ordinary uniforms, making it difficult to find sufficient stowage space. The Japanese Navy had been built on the assumption that the southern tropical seas would be its battleground, and therefore it was inevitable that the supply of equipment for operations in the far north had fallen short of requirements.

Among the troubles which submarines have to face is the difficulty in getting below the surface when submerging in rough weather, as the hull is thrown upward by the waves. With a beam sea it is not difficult but the boat may list up to forty or fifty degrees, for while submerging it has no power to right itself. This may be dangerous, besides causing confusion on board. Conditions usually right themselves at a depth of about ninety feet. In very rough weather, however, rolling may be felt down to one hundred and eighty feet. Fog, too, is the bugbear of submarine navigators. In foggy conditions when the bows of one's own ship are invisible, not even the Japanese Navy's special binoculars were of any avail. Within the boat it is abnormally humid and the condensed moisture drips and trickles everywhere.

The Japanese submarines which operated in northern waters included the new boat I-26, which carried out a reconnaissance of Kiska, Dutch Harbor, and Adak Channel between November 25 and 30, 1941, immediately before the outbreak of war. She was followed by submarines I-174 and 175 which left Kwajalein in the South Seas at the end of January, 1942, for a reconnaissance of the Aleutians, which included patrols off Unalaska Island, Amukta Island, Atka Island, and the vicinity of Kiska. They returned to home waters during mid-February.

The 1st Submarine Squadron comprising I-9, 15, 17,

19, 25, and 26 under the command of Rear Admiral Yamazaki carried out preliminary patrols in the Aleutians prior to May, 1942, in preparation for the invasion of strong points in the Aleutian group. These submarines pressed on with the task of reconnaissance making use of fog-free days or the short nights, when darkness lasted only two or three hours.

I-25 carried out an air reconnaissance of Kodiak, sighting a cruiser and two destroyers. I-26 sighted what were apparently two heavy cruisers while on passage from Alaska Bay to Seattle. The remainder of the squadron provided reconnaissance reports of Dutch Harbor and other places, while awaiting the attacks of the main Japanese forces, which made a successful landing on Attu in June, 1942. Meanwhile submarines I-25 and 26 had each sunk a transport. The whole squadron returned to home ports at the end of June. They were relieved by the 2nd Submarine Squadron comprising I-1, 2, 3, 4, 5, 6, and 7, which operated in these waters until early August of the same year. The fogs were very severe during the end of June and early July, making patrol conditions very difficult, but in mid-July I-7 managed to sink a transport to the south of the Unimak Passage.

The Northern Ocean Base Force Submarine Squadron, then newly organized, was equipped with the older medium-type submarines of the RO class which had been used for the nearer South Sea operations at the beginning of the war. These boats were hardly able to stand up to the rough weather in the northern seas but they were entrusted with the defense of Kiska and took up their stations early in August, 1942. Most of the captains of these boats had passed through the Submarine Commanding Officer's course with me. We met just before they sailed from Yokosuka and none were in good spirits, for they were apprehensive lest their boats would break up in the rough northern weather.

On August 28, 1942, one of our aircraft sighted an enemy force including a cruiser at Nazan on Atka Island, and submarines and flying boats were ordered to attack. Submarines RO-61, 62, and 64 made for Nazan and on August 31, RO-61, commanded by Lieutenant Tokutomi, penetrated the bay, scored a hit with one torpedo on a seaplane carrier, and duly made her escape, but was pursued by destroyers and aircraft and unfortunately sunk. RO-61 was an old boat of the L-4 class which operated in World War I and this was the only occasion she had had to attack the enemy. Other boats of a later type also ventured inside the bay and fired torpedoes but were unable to escape the combined surface and air counterattacks. The old boats were unable to dive deeper than about a hundred and twenty-five feet, and, having little time to make their escape after being attacked once they were spotted, there was little hope. To explain more fully: the danger area of a depth charge, that is the distance at which the explosion could damage the submarine's inner hull and cause an influx of water, was from sixty to seventy-five feet. If the depth setting on the depth charge is taken to be ninety feet, a submarine at any depth between one hundred and fifty feet to the surface would be in the danger area. Thus, with a safe diving depth of only a hundred and twenty-five feet, the old RO-class submarines were always vulnerable. In any case the equipment in these old boats was liable to crack up irrespective of depth-charge attacks, and the slightest concussion was quite enough to finish them.

On September 28, 1942, RO-65 dived when being attacked from the air, and came to rest on the sea bottom. She was unable to surface but most of the crew succeeded in escaping. The remainder of the RO-class boats soon had to return to home waters for repairs, leaving the northern force without any submarines.

At the end of the year, two I-class boats which joined the command were assigned the task of harassing the enemy, who was building an aerodrome on Amchitka Island, but the heavy seas made the operation impossible and they had to withdraw.

In February, 1943, the submarine strength was reinforced by I-31, 168, 169, and 171. Despite the heavy seas and icy winds this force persevered with transport work and patrolling until the middle of March. On May 12, when the enemy began landing on Attu Island, a further reinforcement of twelve submarines of the I class arrived. Before this it had been planned to use surface transport for carrying materials for the urgent completion of the shore bases on Kiska and Attu islands, but this operation was so impeded by the enemy that surface craft had to be replaced by submarines after the second attempt failed. I-7 and six other submarines took over the supply work.

On May 12, 1943, when the enemy landed on Attu, submarines I-7, 31, 34, and 35 hastened to the scene of action. At 1:30 P.M. the next day I-31 scored two hits on an enemy warship off Horutu and also reported damage inflicted on a second vessel, class unknown. The following day the same boat attacked a U. S. cruiser, causing severe damage. After this nothing more was heard of her.*

At 6:30 A.M. on May 16, I-35 torpedoed a light cruiser off the north coast of Attu, inflicting grave damage. I-35 was subsequently depth-charged but suffered little damage. I-34 also was depth-charged thirty miles to the west of Attu on May 14 but escaped with only slight damage.

In February, 1943, I took over command of I-158 which was being fitted out for surface radar experiments. Initial trials were not a success, as we were only able to spot the presence of a submarine on the surface at a distance of two thousand yards, either ahead or astern. This same equipment had already been tried out with some success in surface vessels, but certain features of it were not suitable in submarines. While discussions were still proceeding as to whether the equipment should be adopted, in spite of its deficiencies, news came of the American landing at Attu, and two boats of the flotilla sailed immediately for the north. My boat was left behind to undergo further trials with underwater W/T reception. We heard that our sister ship I-157 had run aground. On June 16, in thick fog, she was making for Kiska at fourteen knots on the surface, when she

---

* I-31 was sunk by gunfire from U. S. destroyer *Frazier*, off Kiska on June 13, 1943.

suddenly grounded at the foot of a precipice on enemy territory. She went hard astern but could not shift. The captain gave the order to lighten the boat by jettisoning twelve tons of lubricating oil, six torpedoes, one hundred and thirteen batteries, and seventy-four tons of oil fuel. Even so, it wasn't easy to dispose of the torpedoes and batteries. Normally part of the hull would be opened up when taking batteries in and out, but in this emergency they were broken up for removal. Eventually I-157 got off the reef at 1:20 P.M. the next afternoon and by good fortune returned safely to Kure on the 26th. She was of course unable to dive but no enemy was encountered en route. Had she been equipped with radar, the accident would have been avoided.

The other submarines operating in this area in foggy conditions without radar continued their game of blindman's buff. They were unable to reap any harvest against American ships which had efficient radar equipment.

Three submarines out of the seventeen attached to the Northern Force were employed in withdrawal operations from Kiska. They made no less than thirteen trips and evacuated a total of eight hundred and twenty men from Kiska to the Kuril Islands. They also landed a hundred and twenty-five tons of equipment and ammunition and a hundred tons of provisions on Kiska during the evacuation.

Meanwhile submarine I-24, in which I had served at the beginning of the war, received orders to take on board the liaison personnel of the Attu defense force who had escaped to the Chichagof area. She approached the harbor on three separate occasions, but, having found no trace of the party, her orders were canceled and nothing more was heard of her. It was surmised she was sunk off the north coast of Attu during the early part of June.*

Submarine I-9 was lost during her second trip to Kiska on transport operations. We heard after the war that she was sunk in a fog off Kiska by a U. S. antisubmarine vessel on June 10.†

I-7 arrived in Vega Bay at Kiska Island on her third transport operation and was involved in a surface action with an enemy patrol vessel. She was hit in the conning tower and the Officer Commanding Flotilla and the captain were both killed. Then she ran aground inside the bay but got off the next day and made for Yokosuka. However, the following night, June 22, she was fired on by three U. S. destroyers out of the fog. The first lieutenant who had taken over command was killed, and while the boat was making her escape under the command of the gunnery officer she ran aground and became a total loss.‡

It was in fact a fight between the blind and those who could see. The enemy was able to track us down even through the fog and open fire without warning. Enemy

---

* U. S. sources claim that I-24 was sunk off the Admiralty Islands on July 27.

† U. S. patrol craft PC-487 picked up I-9's propeller noises by sonar and then got a radar contact at 750 yards in fog. Five depth charges lifted I-9 to the surface. PC-487 sank her by ramming her twice.

‡ U. S. sources report the initial damage inflicted by destroyer *Monaghan*, on June 22. After refloating, I-7 was escaping when three U. S. patrol craft attacked and forced her ashore again, where she was lost with most of her crew.

shells would find their mark, making us unable to dive with the conning-tower holed. On hearing the fate of I-7, withdrawal operations by submarine were canceled. Destroyers successfully took over these duties. There was consternation in the operations department in Tokyo when reports of this "blind" warfare were studied. Questions were asked as to why the submarines had not been equipped with radar. This resulted in a reversal of policy and all submarines were ordered to be fitted immediately with surface radar. For the rest, submarines I-2, 21, and 109 were all fired on without warning out of the fog, but were able to dive and escape without any damage, subsequently returning safely to harbor.

After the Kiska withdrawal operation, I-2 and 56 were left behind with the northern force and were engaged in destroying lines of communication and patrols. They were greatly handicapped by the low temperature (ten degrees below freezing point) and extremely rough weather. Their hulls received severe damage from the heavy seas and in fact they were hampered more by the weather than the enemy.

Submarine I-2 sank a transport off Amchitka during the middle of November.

A total of six submarines—I-7, 9, 31, 24, RO-61, and 65—were sunk during the northern operations, and submarine successes were four transports, a battleship, two light cruisers, one seaplane carrier, and an unknown vessel. Five midget submarines had been sent to Kiska, but through various causes, including heavy seas, they were damaged and were not put to any good use. Our bases in this area were inadequately equipped and when compared with the special pens in use at German bases could only be described as primitive.* Disregard for defensive measures might be regarded as a traditional strong point of the Japanese Navy, but it also had its grave weaknesses. At the present time, when air power is so predominant, bases without adequate defenses are quite useless in serving their purpose. In fact, under such conditions, the weapons which have had so much time and material devoted to their construction will be utterly wasted.

Crews who had lost their ships joined up with the landing parties ashore and were busily occupied rein-forcing the antiaircraft batteries in the intervals between the fog. With the arrival of autumn, there was fierce competition for good fishing grounds to catch the salmon making their way up the small rivers.

---

* U. S. sources record that at Kiska the Japanese submarines were housed in a shed in full view of reconnaissance planes.

14

THE GILBERTS,

SAIPAN,

AND THE

PHILIPPINES

The situation in the Solomons worsened day by day despite our numerous counterattacks. On November 19, 1943, the cream of the U. S. Pacific Fleet under Admiral Nimitz, the C.-in-C., was dispatched to the Gilberts. Without air support, our forces at Tarawa and Makin were soon engaged in a forlorn struggle. The

Americans sent a division of marines to both Makin and Tarawa, and their supporting naval and air forces carried out bombardments and bombing of such intensity that these alone could have overthrown the whole islands. Our forces were no match for the enemy's superior strength, and by November 25 all were wiped out. Submarines I-169, 175, 35, 19, and 39, which were in course of withdrawal from a position three hundred miles southwest of Pearl Harbor, were ordered to the Gilberts at high speed on the surface, and four other boats were also ordered to the rescue. It was this type of operation, repeated time and again regardless of loss, which eventually resulted in the dissipation of our submarine fleet. On this occasion only three of the nine boats returned safely to base. Of these, submarine I-175 sank the U. S. aircraft carrier *Liscomb Bay* and returned safely to her base after evading an antisubmarine-sweeping operation carried out by several destroyers.

I-174, which was on transport operations in the New Guinea area, also received instructions to proceed to the Gilberts on the night of November 26, 1943. She spotted an aircraft light while charging batteries, and immediately crash-dived. The presence of aircraft was apparent for about three hours, but no attack developed. Then the sound faded out, and after waiting another half-hour I-174 surfaced. It was a clear, moonless night. The boat was charging as she cruised along, emitting dim black smoke. At about 8 P.M. the lookout spotted a white bow wave about three hundred yards away and shouted "Destroyer!" I-174 crash-dived again. At ninety feet a depth-charge attack began, which made the boat shudder and put all the lights out. The switchboard was damaged and the power failed. The air blow had to be used to prevent the boat from diving deep. Air bubbles rising to the surface provided a good target and the enemy intensified his attack. There was a lot of water in both the engine and motor rooms. To preserve the trim of the boat and prevent the motors from being flooded, water was shifted from the motor room to the engine room by hand in empty oil drums. Then the batteries and air supply gave out and there was nothing to do but to come to the surface and fight it out. Two minutes after surfacing an aircraft appeared. I-174 dived again, using, as a final resort, all the compressed air in the torpedoes. When she surfaced again, the aircraft was still about, but a friendly squall provided sufficient cover to enable the submarine to escape.

After returning to base the captain made his report to the Admiral Commanding Submarines, in the course of which he remarked that it was just plain suicide for submarines without radar, which could only continue submerged for forty hours at a speed of two to three knots, to operate against the enemy's light forces composed of destroyers and aircraft working in conjunction with antisubmarine-sweeping units. The admiral, however, disagreed, saying that even though boats failed to return, they were playing their part just the same.

Nevertheless, there is no doubt that our submarines were at a serious disadvantage during the two years they had to operate against an enemy equipped with efficient radar. There was just nothing we could do against a sudden attack and many boats were sacrificed needlessly. Much-needed improvements, including increased battery endurance, quick-charging methods, and the fitting of radar, failed to materialize.

In May, 1944, I-45 received orders to lie in wait for the enemy eastward of the Marshall Islands, and she passed at high speed through the Bungo Channel to her objective.

One morning, while cruising on the surface, the captain, who was resting, suddenly heard the officer of the watch calling, "Crash-dive." Almost immediately the boat was being bombed by an aircraft which appeared out of the clouds. The boat was not yet submerged before she was hit astern. The impact was accompanied by a terrible shaking which seemed to lift the boat. She lay crippled with her bows upward above the surface. Then the enemy opened fire with machine guns. Determined to save the submarine, the captain tried diving while going slow astern. This did the trick, and she started to submerge, though she lay at an angle of seven degrees. Down she went, to four hundred and fifty feet. At this depth the water pressure buckled the plates in the after-part of the inner pressure hull. The order to blow the main ballast was given to stop her going down further, but the air bubbles rising to the surface gave the enemy a good target for more bombs. Fortunately the crew was able to keep her down to three hundred feet, where they stuck it out all day till sunset. Under cover of darkness I-45 surfaced to inspect the damage. There was a large hole in the stern which left no choice but to turn back for Yokosuka for repairs. The journey passed without incident until she reduced speed on entering Tokyo Bay. There, in the midst of the antisubmarine nets, the rudder failed to function, but after some hair-raising experiences she got clear and arrived safely to Yokosuka. Inspection in dry dock showed that all the rudder plates were gone except the bottom one. I-45 was lucky to have got back at all in such a condition.

Before the enemy actually made his attack on Saipan Island, many opinions were advanced as to the probable locality of the attack, but intelligence failed to provide reliable information. The landings took place on June 15, 1944. Submarines ordered to concentrate in the Saipan area were late in taking up their attacking positions. During the latter half of May, 1944, eight submarines, RO-109, 108, 112, 104, 105, 106, 116, and I-44, took up positions one hundred and fifty miles to the north of Admiralty Island to counter the move of the U. S. forces along the New Guinea coast toward Biak and Palau. The enemy were well versed in the tactics to be used against our submarines. Having sighted a single vessel, they would take up positions to hunt the rest one by one and keep them submerged. On this occasion, one of our submarines was sighted on her arrival in the patrol area, and in consequence all the others were subject to attack by air and sea when they reached their appointed positions. RO-109 was depth-charged for a whole day. At this juncture information was received from submarine H.Q. that the enemy was fully aware of the dispositions of all the submarines taking part in the operation. RO-109 and 108, acting independently, immediately altered course to take up positions some hundred miles away and were saved, but the remaining five RO-class boats were overwhelmed and sunk.

I-44, which was the first submarine to have been fitted with radar, still survived. She had been ordered to proceed to the north of Admiralty Island, and left Kure on May 15 to take up her station. While cruising on the surface at night, constantly using her radar, she was suddenly bombed. The officer of the watch immediately gave the order to dive, but when the boat surfaced later more aircraft appeared and attacked. There was nothing showing on the radar set though the bomb explosions were quite audible. The boat therefore had to continue submerged. During the night, while all were asleep, there was a depth-charge attack which put the depth gauge out of action. There was water in nearly all compartments. By this time it was eleven o'clock in the forenoon and only an hour's battery power was left. The first lieutenant was a spirited individual and advocated surfacing and fighting it out, as there was nothing to be gained by remaining submerged with uncharged batteries. The captain was persuaded and the order was given to prepare for a gun action and to make ready the machine guns and revolvers. A periscope inspection revealed a flying boat passing by and a destroyer waiting. At that moment a heavy squall blew up. This was an opportunity not to be missed, and I-44 surfaced and, leaving the destroyer astern, made off at full speed to the northwest. About an hour later, while proceeding on the surface with all the armament manned, a four-engined flying boat appeared. However, it flew on without attacking, while the captain stood munching a biscuit on the bridge. When close to Saipan, I-44 attempted to dive, but the vents would not open and they had to get her down by opening the lower pressure distributor valve. Thus she survived to fight another day.

Shortly after this the enemy attack on Saipan developed and all available submarines were ordered to concentrate in the area. RO-115, on patrol off Palau, altered course forthwith for Saipan at high speed. By June 19 she had reached a position fifty miles to the west of Rota Island, and was making her way on the surface through waters well guarded by enemy naval planes when she was severely bombed, the nearest bomb landing about forty yards away. However, she continued on her way undamaged. Next a large enemy force appeared and RO-115 had to dive again. She spent some considerable time trying to locate a group of aircraft carriers, and at last in the evening she caught up with them. It was after sunset when she got through the destroyer screen and fired four torpedoes at a *Wasp*-class carrier. The results, however, were not observed, for RO-115 immediately went down to two hundred and fifty feet. Unfortunately, she did not escape being bombed. The boat started to leak and half the lights went out, but luckily things did not get any worse. She was then ordered to retire to Truk, having expended all her torpedoes. On her arrival there she found that RO-113, 114, 109, and I-5 had already preceded her.

When the enemy attack on Guam developed, RO-114

was ordered to make a detour of the island and attack the enemy, but nothing more was heard of her after she reported an attack on a large warship.

Submarines I-55, 45, and 26 sailed from Yokosuka for Guam carrying tanks, guns, ammunition, but only I-26 achieved her object, and nothing further was heard of I-55. I-45 returned to Yokosuka after abandoning the operation because the securing wires of the tank she was carrying on deck were carried away and the tank fell into the sea. I-26 succeeded in getting her tank to Guam, which was then surrounded by the enemy. Having reached the prearranged position for landing it, when still submerged she appeared to run aground and came to a dead stop. The captain asked the navigator to confirm the exact position. He indicated a shoal to the southwest of the island, on which they were probably aground. They waited until nearly sunset, keeping periscope watch. Then they started the engines and I-26 began to move astern, scraping along the bottom. Eventually they rose to periscope depth. Inspection revealed the edge of a rock which was the mark for the prearranged landing position. The navigator had miscalculated and the boat had actually grounded on the landing position itself! Having accomplished her mission, I-26 slipped through the enemy cordon and returned to Yokosuka.

In the period covering the battle for Saipan thirteen submarines were lost: RO-111, 114, 44, 42, 36, 48, 117, I-185, 184, 10, 6, 5, and 55. I-44, 41, 38, 26, 45, RO-109, 115, 113, and 112 returned safely to base. It was at this time that our submarines were at last being equipped with radar. Only one third of those so fitted were damaged, while, of those without, two thirds were lost, thus clearly illustrating the value of this equipment.

At the end of August, 1944, submarine I-165 was rushed to Korim Bay on Biak Island, which was isolated and partly occupied by the enemy. She was to act as a link between our remaining forces on the island and to take off the Air Officer Commanding. She had embarked all manner of stores, including yeast, torches, ammunition, and medical stores, in addition to sixty drums containing provisions which were stowed on the upper deck.

One afternoon, when the island was clearly in sight on the horizon, I-165 sighted three enemy torpedo craft. She dived but was depth-charged, and at three hundred and twenty-five feet the inner hull began to emit strange creaking sounds and cracks appeared in the paint. She was an old boat and the pressure of water was having its effect. The captain at once brought her up to three hundred feet, and she proceeded to dodge her pursuers, using her underslung rudder gear. However, the enemy torpedo craft maintained pursuit. Perhaps some of the drums on the upper deck had carried away and risen to the surface, thus giving away the boat's position. The hunt continued for over a day and night. The captain decided to release all the drums and take flight. Even so, the enemy continued his depth-charge attacks. Oil was prevented from leaking to the surface by operating the special equipment fitted for this purpose, but there was damage to the interior of the boat aft, and more and more water was coming in. The water collecting in the motor room was transferred to the torpedo compartment by means of a chain of buckets, but the stern of the boat continued to sink. The temperature inside the boat had risen to one hundred and fifty degrees, and finally all the oxygen was released to make it possible to breathe. The remaining food supplies also were given out and everyone allowed his fill, as one and all had quite resolved to face the end, which now seemed inevitable. That night, however, the enemy gave up the chase. At 10 P.M. I-165 surfaced and made for Amboina at her best possible speed. Examination in the harbor revealed that the after auxiliary rudder was badly bent and that there was other serious damage.

Submarines I-10 and 38 made every effort to extricate the staff of the Submarine Fleet H.Q. from Saipan, but were unable to achieve this. At length, one day in June, a signal was received from the Admiral Commanding Submarines announcing that he, his staff, and the midget submarine personnel were making a dash for it, and the command was abolished. As a temporary measure the Officer Commanding the 7th Submarine Squadron at Yokosuka took over.

On October 20, 1944, the American forces began landings on Leyte Island. The remnants of our submarine fleet had been ordered to concentrate in the Philippines area on October 11. In all there were eleven submarines: RO-46, 43, 41, I-53, 38, 46, 41, 26, 45, 54, and 56.

Though the enemy was sighted frequently, only I-56

succeeded in getting in an attack. Using her radar, she spotted the presence of a large force on October 22 and that night she met with an enemy convoy. Having slipped through the destroyer screen, she attacked and sank an enemy transport with three torpedoes. On October 25, while approaching Leyte, her radar once more showed the presence of enemy craft and she dived immediately. She penetrated into a group of U. S. aircraft carriers and fired a salvo of five torpedoes at one of them, hearing the sound of three hits. One of these torpedoes appeared to have accounted for one of the destroyer screen. A severe depth-charge attack followed which continued intermittently for some hours. The engine room was partially flooded and the lights went out. The captain quelled the resultant panic by calmly demanding to know the precise cause for the flooding. This was found to be due to the loosening of a valve. The boat remained submerged for twenty-four hours and when she surfaced in the pitch dark, an unexploded depth charge was found resting on the after part of the upper deck! It was shaped like a thirty-kg. bomb and was carefully taken back to Kure dockyard. Six other submarines stationed in the Leyte area failed to return. Submarine I-41 reported sinking a transport and an *Essex*-class aircraft carrier off the east coast of the Philippines on October 27 and November 3 respectively. Subsequently submarines RO-49, 50, 41, 43, 109, and 112 were stationed off the east coast of the Philippines from mid-November to mid-December. During this period RO-50 reported sinking an aircraft carrier and a destroyer.

In early January, 1945, when the U. S. forces made their landing in Lingayen Gulf, RO-45 made an attack on an *Idaho*-class battleship on January 12 and RO-46 sank two transports west of Iba. RO-50 sank a transport to the southeast of Surigao on February 1, while RO-109 scored two hits on each of an aircraft carrier, a cruiser, and a destroyer off the west coast of Lingayen Gulf on January 17. Submarines RO-112, 113, and 115 were ordered to carry out transport work between Takao (in Formosa) and the northern tip of Luzon but were all sunk between February 10 and 13.*

---

* U. S. sources claim that RO-115 was sunk on January 31, 1945.

15

RADAR—

THE KEY

TO VICTORY

The turning point in the submarine war came when all enemy ships and aircraft were fitted with efficient radar sets. I have already quoted many examples of the way our own submarines were handicapped by having no radar. Here are some of my own experiences.

Submarine RO-44, of which I was captain, completed

her fitting out and began trials in September, 1943. At the time fitting submarines with air radar had scarcely been considered. During our trials with surface radar I had spoken with Captain Ito of the Naval Technical Department, who told me that he had pressed for the immediate fitting of a set, then in existence, which had a range of about eight thousand yards. Knowing that the Ministry of Marine authorities was somewhat lackadaisical despite knowledge of front-line conditions, he had urged the Staff Officer of the 11th Submarine Squadron to go up to Tokyo to press the matter personally. Unfortunately this officer was transferred elsewhere just when he had obtained permission for the Tokyo visit, so nothing more came of the proposal. Matters just couldn't be left as they were so I asked to be allowed to go myself, but this was not approved. At this point I went to see a radar set said to be in use at the Kure Naval Air Station. It was portable and easily capable of being fitted in a submarine. I came rushing back and persuaded the Staff Officer Submarines to ask the captain of the Naval Air Station to lend it to us. He gladly gave his approval, and late one Saturday afternoon we brought it over on a truck from the Kure dockyard electrical department. It was tested out and adjusted on the Sunday and placed on board by the time we left harbor for trials on the Monday.

That day, November 13, I got the Kure Naval Air Station to send out a target aircraft and RO-44 was excused from other exercises in order to carry our radar trials. We started off in the calm conditions of Ise Bay. The set proved to be very inaccurate. When the target aircraft developed engine trouble we had to abandon testing that day. The next day there were ideal flying conditions and we started out again early in the morning. This time reception was good for distances from five to six thousand to a maximum of fourteen thousand yards. True, these were not exceptional results, but even so, they were a great improvement on our previous helpless state. An urgent signal, supported by the senior officer of 11th Submarine Squadron, was sent to the proper authorities stating the results of the trials. This brought back a reply asking why trials had been carried out without the approval of the Naval Technical Department. All hope of action subsequently faded away.

I tried again to get permission to go to Tokyo with plans for radar to be fitted in RO-class submarines, but couldn't get approval for the trip. Meanwhile, we were about to leave for Maizuru to make final preparations for active service. This meant that we left the 11th Submarine Squadron and joined the 6th (Submarine) Fleet. I persisted with my request to visit Tokyo and at last it was approved, and I had a chance of expressing my views at a Naval Technical Department meeting. The senior member present proceeded to bring up a number of objections and said that new equipment, designed by the Technical Department, would soon be ready and we'd better wait till then. As it happened the radar set designed by the Naval Technical Department had been under test at Kure dockyard. The senior technician there had told me there was no prospect of early action, and this was what prompted me to carry out trials in RO-44! Anyway I could get no satisfactory answer and the meeting decided to shelve the matter. This was most unsatisfactory, so, refusing to be put off, I went the next day to the Technical Research Bureau, where I was received much more enthusiastically. We went into all the technical difficulties and were able to reach workable solutions. Thus armed, I put in a second appearance at the Naval Technical Department and tried to carry my point, but the Research Bureau's solution was not accepted. I think it was a case of interdepartmental jealousy. I had no time to argue any further for I had to return to Maizuru. All I had succeeded in getting was approval for the increased allotment of one pair of binoculars for lookout purposes! It was indeed regrettable that our Headquarters Staff were more concerned with preserving their dignity than giving proper appreciation to active service conditions.

Soon afterward, at the end of December, we left for the southern battle area, still without radar. Our course took us through the Bungo Channel and as this was a favorite spot for lurking enemy submarines, we made what speed we could by night and dived each day at dawn. The thought of having to cruise submerged when so close to Japanese waters was not a pleasant one, but such were the hard facts of war. The second night at sea brought us beyond the danger area and after that we cruised entirely on the surface. At that time all was well in the Marshalls and at Rabaul, and as far as Truk we could anticipate no worries from enemy aircraft. We passed New Year's Day, 1944, at sea, and only ten days after leaving the blizzards of Maizuru, we were basking in tropical heat. We reached Truk in early January. It was a grand sight to see the *Yamato* and the greater part of the combined fleet at anchor. I reported forthwith to the C.-in-C. 6th Fleet and described my efforts to get air radar to the Senior Staff Officer. I-185 had left Japan on operations at the same time as we and had gone to Rabaul where her captain had made a similar report to the C.-in-C. SE. Area Fleet. Fortunately there was a spare aircraft radar set available and I-185 promptly had it fitted. The results it gave were better than those obtained when I tried out the same equipment in RO-44. This was duly signaled to all concerned. The Chief of Staff himself flew to Tokyo to raise the matter yet again. Again, to our great regret, no immediate decision to so equip the submarines was taken. The submarine crews in the forward area were longing for radar as farmers look for rain in a long drought. In theory submarines should refrain as much as possible from using their radar for fear of its being picked up by the enemy, and use instead a special receiving set for picking up the enemy's transmissions. There were many, even among submarine captains, who subscribed to this theory, but the majority were in favor of the more positive method of using their own radar rather than depending on the comparatively few opportunities presented for picking up enemy signals. The latter method was a complete failure in the Kiska operations.

In actual fact, the only radar receiver fitted in our boats was one we had acquired from the Germans. Thus we had been reduced to rely on foreign tuition. What was the reason for such a disgraceful state of affairs?

Was it due to a deficiency in our scientific knowledge and in our electrical industry? Unhappily this was precisely the case. Though we were poor, would it not have been better to have devoted more of our resources to scientific research? As we were deficient both in the bare necessities of life and natural resources, we should have diverted more of our national income into scientific research. Our scientific research policy was based on principles long since out of date—and the blindness of our submarines was the inevitable outcome. At Guadalcanal Island, U. S. aircraft would bomb a submarine on sight either by night or day without waiting to identify it. No doubt U. S. submarines with their up-to-date radar were confident of being able to submerge before being sighted by any aircraft. Thus a U. S. aircraft coming upon a submarine idly cruising on the surface would assume that it must be one of those deaf and blind Japanese! In our despair we were almost driven to the view that a single radar set would be of more value than a hundred submarines.

On May 15, 1944, I relinquished command of RO-44 just before she left Kure. My next job was to take charge of fitting out submarine I-58. I was due for about a month's leave; but, not feeling the need for it, I instead devoted myself wholeheartedly to following up my ideas about radar. When I reported at the 6th Fleet H.Q., recently withdrawn from Truk, I came across a staff paper advocating the removal of the "useless" surface radar sets. To my astonishment the author of this fantastic opinion turned out to be the Admiral Commanding Submarines! In view of my early experiences with radar in I-58 I was very interested. I had heard nothing of more recent trials. As RO-44 had no radar, I was unable to refrain from commenting on the Admiral's paper:

> It is premature to remove this useful equipment—indeed it would be a retrograde step. Why, when the set is fitted in submarines, is it regarded as useless, while the same set is still in use in surface craft? If further investigation shows that it really is valueless, then it can be removed. In my view, there is still plenty of scope for the submarine's crew to improve the set's performance, and I request therefore that the decision to remove the radar equipment be deferred until I-58 is completed.

I then visited the personnel department of the Kure Naval Base and explained that the cause of failure in submarine electrical equipment was mainly due to the absence of skilled electricians in the crew. During the year and a half in which radar sets had been tried out, no high-grade electricians had been drafted to the submarines in question. After some argument I persuaded the personnel department to send me two expert electricians for I-58. Then I went round to the dockyard and, after carrying out exhaustive research with an experienced radar technical officer, we devised what we felt would be the best method for fitting this set into a submarine.

At length I received orders to join I-58, and went to Yokosuka to take up my appointment. While I was going round the dockyard making myself known to the various officials, I urged all and sundry not to be late in fitting her new equipment. This involved the new method of fit-

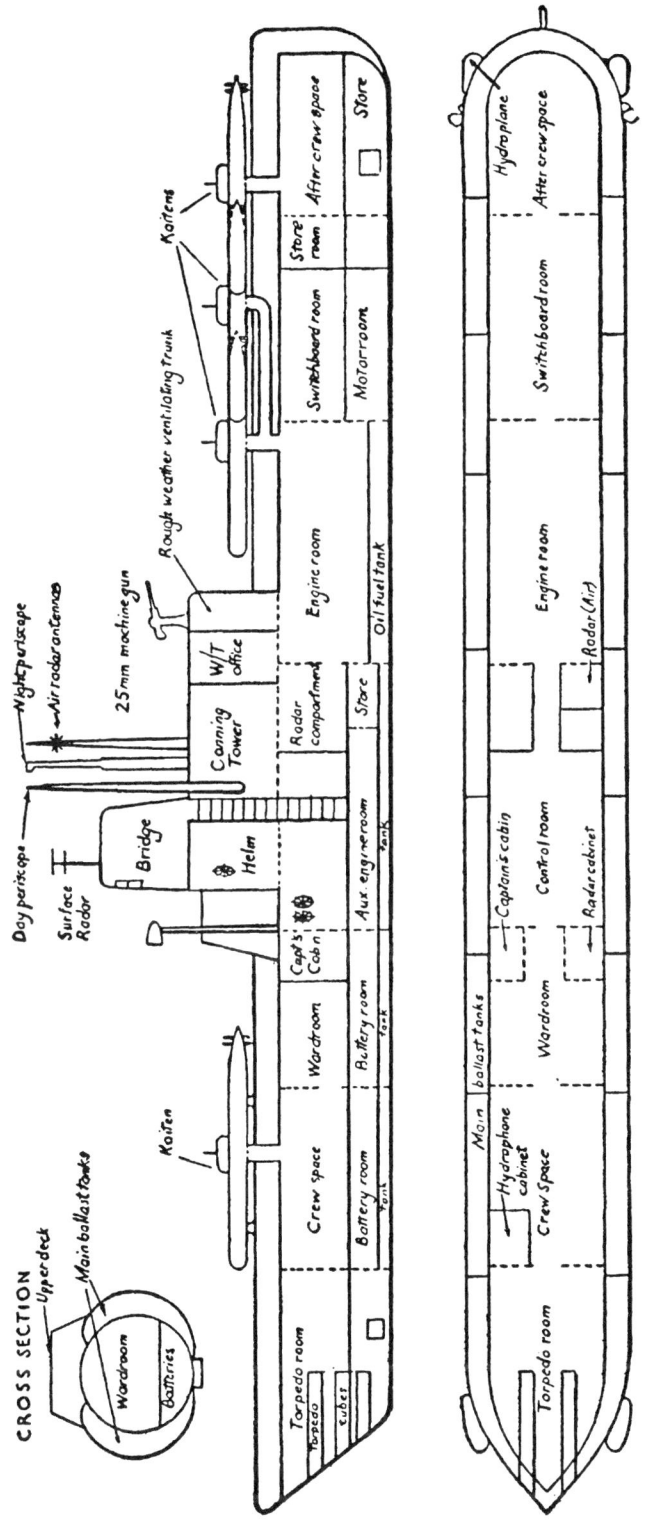

CROSS SECTION

Upper deck

Main ballast tanks

Wardroom

batteries

Torpedo

Torpedo room

tuber

Kaiten

Battery room tank

Crew space

Wardroom

Battery room tank

Cap't's Cabin

Aux engine room tank

Helm

Bridge

Day periscope

Night periscope

Surface Radar

Air radar antenna

25mm machine gun

Coning Tower

Radar compartment

Store

W/T office

Engine room

Oil fuel tank

Rough weather ventilating trunk

Kaitens

Switchboard room

Motor room

Store room

After crew space

Store

Torpedo room

Main ballast tanks

Hydrophone cabinet

Crew space

Wardroom

Captain's cabin

Control room

Radar cabinet

Engine room

Radar (Air)

Switchboard room

After crew space

Hydroplane

I-54-class submarine, equipped to carry Kaitens. I-58, the author's command, was of this class. (Not to scale.)

ting the surface radar set as well as one or two items concerning alterations to the machine-gun mounting. But in both cases the officials concerned, while expressing regrets, seemed unable to get the work done and I had to enlist the support of the Naval Technical Department and the Research Bureau to get things as I wanted them. Perhaps in my anxiety I hurt the dignity of the dockyard officials, but there was a war which allowed no time for haggling. In peacetime, one would have left everything to the dockyard staff, but in all the circumstances I have no regrets for my actions, for both my ship and I were in danger of being sent to the bottom. The dockyard officials at first refused to compromise over the manner of fitting the radar set, and I had further endless trouble before eventually getting them to install the equipment my way. The high-grade radar artificer promised by the personnel department took a long time in coming but eventually turned up in January after I had sent three hasteners on the subject. Apparently the signal school had tried to hang on to the man because they were short of instructors.

The battle for Saipan started while we were fitting out, and many of the submarines which went to operate there and off Guam failed to return. The fall of Saipan was a mortal blow. With it the air attacks on Tokyo began.

I-58 was approaching completion and we reached the stage of deep-diving trials. The normal safe diving depth was three hundred feet, but I-58 was designed to withstand the pressure of water up to four hundred and fifty feet. This was very necessary in wartime to evade depth-charge attacks. I-58's diving trials were carried out to three hundred feet.

In diving trials a marker buoy was towed astern to indicate the boat's positions and kept a check on her while submerged. First, measurements were taken in several places on the diameter of the pressure hull as she lay on the surface. Then the boat dived and measurements were continued every thirty feet to determine the extent of compression of the hull. Leakage points and discharge pump capacities were then tested and, all being well, I-58 surfaced, similar measurements being taken every thirty feet as she rose. Finally we had to ascertain whether she returned exactly to her predive conditions, when she reached the surface.

In actual fact, on the first trial, a bad leak developed at two hundred feet, and the trial was abandoned, but the next day the trouble was put right and we started again. This time everything went without a hitch. Most of the naval training establishments were situated near Yokosuka and it was therefore a convenient locality for the training of submarine personnel. I had the lookouts and engine-room ratings put through special courses and the standard was very high.

In all I saw three submarines built during the war, and I was much struck by the greater efficiency of the private yards as compared to the naval dockyards, which didn't seem to care how much time and money they wasted.

At length I-58 was commissioned and proceeded to the Inland Sea to join the training squadron for final working-up.

After the war the Americans said that the closest co-operation between air and surface vessels was essential in the efficient conduct of antisubmarine operations and that both should normally be centralized under a single command. The worst experiences that our submarines had to undergo was that of prolonged depth-charge attacks by destroyers and smaller vessels combined with bombing from the air. Such attacks were frequent subsequent to August, 1942, when the Americans began their night attacks using radar, for we had no means to counteract them. In fact from this time on we continued to suffer crippling losses from U. S. antisubmarine tactics, all through the battles of Makin and Tarawa and the latter half of the Solomons campaign in 1943 and the battles of Admiralty Island, Saipan, the Philippines, and Okinawa in 1944-45.

If a submarine remains submerged for more than forty hours it must surface long enough to change the air. Then, again, even though fully charged, batteries will not last longer than a similar period. When the boat has to dive with batteries not fully charged she cannot remain submerged so long. Success was sometimes achieved by remaining stopped and keeping at the required depth by taking in or pumping out a small quantity of water from the tanks—this, of course, economized in battery power. Nevertheless, the batteries would still eventually run down and many times our submarines were forced to surface close to the enemy. Sometimes our submarines were sighted while surfaced to recharge and would be severely depth-charged when crash-diving to escape. Some were saved by remaining down for a long period, but eventually most of them had to surface and fight it out with the waiting enemy. Sometimes there was insufficient high-pressure air for these emergency dives, and air had to be taken from the torpedoes. This meant the submarine was unarmed, for the high-pressure air cylinders used to fire the torpedoes couldn't be refilled without surfacing.

Thus there was no method of overcoming this weakness whereby a submarine was compelled to resurface after forty hours, and in most cases the only boats to make their escape in these circumstances were those favored with the friendly protection of squalls or other natural aids.

The Americans achieved great success with their own submarines against ours. We were surprised after the war to hear the figures of losses inflicted by U. S. submarines. In fact, losses due to air attack were comparatively few. This was due perhaps to bad marksmanship by the aircraft—though the number of attacks was high, few hits resulted in fatal damage.

16

HUMAN

TORPEDOES

The idea of obtaining a certain hit by torpedoes fired from a submarine but driven by a volunteer took shape at the time of the first Japanese attack on Pearl Harbor, when five midget submarines were employed. Several tiny submarines were built for trials carried out on an island known under the code name of "Base P," near Kure Naval Base.

By January, 1943, the "human torpedo" project had reached the stage when designs could be put forward. The first of these involved certain death for the operator, a fact which the Japanese naval authorities were not prepared to accept. A device was therefore added which, on pressing a button some hundred and fifty feet before reaching the target, threw the operator into the sea. The prototype put up to the Naval Staff in about February, 1944, was accepted. These suicide weapons offered the hope of compensating in part for the heavy reversals being sustained at that time: Saipan Island had already fallen to the enemy and many heavy losses had been suffered. Although there were considerable doubts as to the success or failure of this new weapon, it was named "Kaiten," which means "the turn toward heaven," and in this mood of anxious hope, construction began at the Kure dockyard torpedo experimental depot.

While this was going on a trials base was established in Tokuyama Bay with a rear admiral to command a unit embracing all small-type submarine training.

Alas! on the first day's trials, one of the principal advocates of this type of craft who had volunteered for the job went to his death in Tokuyama Bay, together with his cooperator: the nose of the boat stuck in the mud and it could not be surfaced. This boded ill for the future of the new weapon.

Nevertheless, frenzied training was carried out for two months, and on November 8, 1944, the Kikumizu unit was formed and left for operations. The human torpedoes were split up between three parent submarines, I-36, 47, and 37, the first two proceeding to Ulithi and I-37 to the Kossol Passage near Palau Island.

I-36 and I-47 made the approach to Ulithi according to plan on November 19. Reconnaissance confirmed that a large U. S. force of over a hundred vessels, including aircraft carriers, battleships, and other craft were at anchor. The human torpedoes were launched at 4:30 A.M. on the 20th, one from I-36 and four from I-47. The senior officer of the unit, whose torpedo was launched from I-47, was one of the strongest advocates of the use of this weapon, and before his departure he left behind him the following message:

> Daylight observation disclosed over a hundred ships at anchor in Ulithi. Though this provides a golden opportunity for the use of our human torpedoes, there are but two submarines and eight human torpedoes—a very regrettable matter.

At the time of launching he carried in his pocket a photograph of his fellow officer, killed during the trials, and on this, his first operation, showed great firmness of purpose. Before embarking he expressed his gratitude to the captain of I-47 for having confirmed the enemy strength and brought the boat to the most favorable position for launching. He wished I-47 a long life and with a firm handshake he embarked in his torpedo, saying, "Thank you for all your help. Give my regards to the boats that follow me." Alas! Nothing was ever heard of the results he achieved, nor was his fate known.

I-36 and 47 returned safely to Kure on December

1, but I-37, which had proceeded to Palau, failed to return.

Although the results achieved by the Kikumizu unit had not been ascertained, much was expected of the Kaiten, and a further unit, the Kongo unit, was formed with the six remaining large submarines of the latest type.

The instructions issued for this unit called for I-36 to proceed to Ulithi, I-47 to Hollandia, I-56 to Admiralty Island, I-53 to Palau, and I-58, the boat I commanded, to Guam Island; all were to attack on January 11, 1945. I-48 was to attack Ulithi later on January 20.

Fifteen of us had graduated in the submarine course at the naval college, but by this time most of my class had been killed in action and there were only five of us left. Oddly enough, of the six submarines in the Kongo unit, five were commanded by the remaining five members of my class.

The Kaitens had been built in conditions of great secrecy, but we knew they had already been used in the first attack on Ulithi. An officer operating one of them wrote:

> The future use of human torpedoes will be fraught with difficulty. The more we use our opportunities for attack the more must we pay careful attention to the method of employment of this craft.

In other words, it had to be assumed that the Americans were aware of this form of attack, so we could expect that, after the second attack, our adversary would be well on his guard. Thus both the approach of the submarine to the launching position and the actual penetration of the Kaiten to its target became a much more hazardous affair. And so, in fact, it proved.

My own submarine, I-58, having completed preparations at Sasebo, proceeded to Kure to take in fuel, provisions, and torpedoes. On December 29 she sailed for the human torpedo base where all ranks were addressed by the Admiral Commanding Submarines. We took a photograph to commemorate the occasion, and after a grand send-off I-58 left harbor in company with I-36 and 53, accompanied also by a host of crowded motor boats whose occupants were chanting in unison the names of the personnel of the departing unit. The human torpedo pilots were sitting in their respective craft, wearing white towels round their heads and brandishing their swords.

On board the submarine, the mark I-58 had been erased and replaced by the Kongo unit badge. At the masthead, beside the ensign we flew a flag bearing the inscription, "The unpredictable Kaiten."

We passed through the Bungo Channel and turned south, proceeding on the surface. Through the evening haze we took a dramatic farewell look at the homeland; then even the outlying islands disappeared far beyond the horizon.

Enemy submarines were at large in the area, so a strict lookout was necessary. We commenced zigzagging and proceeded through the night at increased speed. We were using for the first time an antiaircraft radar set, but although it had been adjusted while in sight of land, we found it wasn't working very well. A man had to be sent on deck to make some repairs as we were particularly anxious not to be spotted. The night passed, and it was the first of January, 1945. The boat was getting some help from the northwest trade winds. The sunrise that morning at sea was indeed a magnificent sight. Alcoholic drinks were normally forbidden at sea, but this was a special occasion, so permission was given to serve enough *sake* to drink toasts. After the boat had dived, cheers for the Emperor could be given and toasts drunk without any qualms.

During the voyage to the target the two Kaiten officer pilots were always together for meals, but the warrant officers messed with the crew and we didn't normally see them. Today, however, they were summoned to the wardroom and we all fed together.

From January 2 we were in range of enemy patrols from Saipan and Guam and we submerged at times when enemy aircraft were expected. This same day, while using the radar set, an enemy aircraft was sighted through binoculars. It was clear that the radar set was still unreliable! The lookouts were accordingly warned to keep a very strict watch for aircraft.

Since its recapture by the Americans, it seemed that Guam had assumed great importance as a Central Pacific base. Even though our present operation wasn't known, we could expect very careful precautions to be taken by the enemy in view of the earlier attack on Ulithi. The best plan, therefore, was to make a detour and approach from a quarter where the defenses could be expected to be light. This involved proceeding further to the south and approaching on a line joining Ulithi and Guam, in other words to make the approach from the enemy quarter. As we were nearing an enemy base, submerged periods grew longer and those on the surface shorter. On January 7 we passed the enemy line of communications between Guam and Ulithi, and we remained a long time submerged, keeping a very strict lookout. There was no question of any submarines in the unit attacking the enemy before launching her human torpedoes; her sole object was to remain hidden.

During long periods submerged there was little to do on board. The two Kaiten pilots had no duties beyond preparing their torpedoes and periscope drill, and they took to playing chess. One of them had been present on the occasion of the Ulithi attack but was unable to take an active part because of a defect in his torpedo. He was a very good chess player. The other was a term mate of our gunnery officer and was fat and composed, sitting astride his torpedo and brandishing his sword.

When he was at the naval college, I can well remember him coming to my submarine (I-58) for training. That was in 1943, so barely two years had passed. The same pupil had now become a sublieutenant and yet he couldn't be more than twenty-one or twenty-two. It was very sad to think he was billed for certain death in this attempt to turn the tide of war. Painful though it was to think of sending out these men on such expeditions, the times were such that the number of those who did not return were growing apace in fields quite outside special units, and both old and young alike were departing from this world. In such a situation, sooner or later, their fate was inevitable.

On the 6th we arrived on the line of communications between Guam and Leyte. At 2 A.M. an aircraft showed up on the radar and we dived and proceeded submerged. Up to now we had managed to dodge enemy aircraft, but now we were near our objective and on the main traffic route, and we might well have met with aircraft unexpectedly. We should have been able to depend on our radar, but it was too unreliable to give due warning. Thus we had to proceed submerged and only surfaced at 2 P.M., which was the time we could expect a gap in the attentions of enemy patrol aircraft.

The weather was fine and calm, with a gentle breeze, and morale was high. Although it was January we were wearing tropical clothing. In the sea we noticed many boxes and empty drums bobbing about. We went cautiously on the surface, alert, expecting to be sighted. Surprisingly we were able to proceed on the surface for an hour and a half during that afternoon, and we charged our batteries and changed the air in the boat before diving at 3:30 P.M. This made up for our having to dive by night. We had decided to surface each day at five o'clock in the afternoon on the supposition that the enemy patrol aircraft reached their farthest position and turned back at about noon. There must have been some truth in this, as we never met with an enemy aircraft then. There is usually an unexpected loophole like this, but it would have been unwise to follow the same procedure all the time on approaching our objective.

That night, January 6, we surfaced at 10 P.M., the time when we reckoned that the enemy night patrol would have returned to base. About 10:30 P.M. several patterns appeared on the radar screen, and the lookout reported a dark object, probably a ship, in the direction of a squall at a range of about one hundred and fifty yards. We dived hastily without stopping to investigate. Nothing was heard on the hydrophones, but we continued submerged. From the next day, the 7th, we surfaced earlier in the day and only once during the night between 9 P.M. and 4 A.M. At last the day of the operation was almost due: it was January 9. Afterward we learned this was the day the enemy began their landing in Lingayen Gulf in Luzon, the main island of the Philippines.

We had been given an air reconnaissance report on Guam, but there was nothing in it about the ships at anchor there, and we were somewhat apprehensive. However, an earlier report had given the ships at anchor as one aircraft carrier and sixty to seventy other vessels, so we had reason to hope that there would be one or two big ones still there. On the 10th we received confirmatory orders from the C.-in-C. to carry out the attack as planned, and I passed on this news to the Kaiten pilots. At about 2 A.M. on the 11th we sighted the exhaust trail of an aircraft passing at short range and we dived. Normally we could estimate the times of arrival and departure of enemy patrol aircraft by listening in on their radio communications wave, and there shouldn't have been one about at this hour. Possibly this one was the Ulithi area communications aircraft. At any rate we had estimated that there shouldn't have been a patrol aircraft on this course. Since the 6th we had sighted many ships and aircraft, but believed that we ourselves had passed unseen. If the enemy had seriously carried out a sweep, we could have offered no resistance. But once again we couldn't place much reliance on our air radar.

At about 9 A.M. on the 11th we heard the sound of the reciprocating engines of what seemed like a merchant ship proceeding unescorted. That was proof that the enemy didn't know about us, and two hours later we reached a position from which Guam should have been just in sight. The periscope was raised cautiously. At first I thought the blur was only a cloud, but closer inspection revealed without doubt that it was Guam. The navigator had done his work splendidly—it was Guam, and we were still twenty-six miles off.

I pointed out the distant target to the Kaiten pilots, and then we dived and made straight for the launching position. From time to time we heard the sound of propellers of probable merchant ships, but all were unescorted. The enemy was quite unsuspecting. At dusk we raised the periscope once more, but could see nothing owing to a squall. At 9 P.M. we sighted a large merchant ship passing close, but we were forbidden to take any action. We were not zigzagging. At supper that night we drank the healths of the Kaiten pilots and toasted to their success.

At 9:43 P.M. we surfaced at an estimated distance of eleven miles to the west of Apra harbor on the island of Guam and made for the launching point at seven knots. A final inspection of the torpedoes was made. Thirteen minutes after surfacing, our W/T officer reported that he had intercepted an enemy message from Guam W/T station, reporting the sighting of a suspicious vessel.

Could this mean I-58? We had still two hours to run so there was nothing to do but to press on.

Our air reconnaissance report of the 9th showed that there were present at Guam twenty large and forty small transports and four floating docks: not much in the way of big prizes. One felt sorry for the human torpedo pilots, but I told them to search for the largest transport, which was heavily loaded, and also explained that the floating dock somewhere in the corner was not without its merits as a target. I also consoled them by saying that an aircraft carrier might have come in since the report was made on the 9th.

One of the officers left behind a statement which I remembered for a long time:

> I wanted all the details of the photographic reconnaissance. Was it not irresponsible to send us into the attack without giving us some idea of the enemy's defenses or the conditions inside the harbor?

Anyway it seemed that the enemy had really sighted us at last. The pilots of Numbers 2 and 3 torpedoes could only embark from the upper deck and I gave the order for them to get into their craft at once for fear of the enemy catching us in the act. It was cloudy but the stars were bright. In the darkness their faces were invisible when the two pilots, wearing shorts, came on the bridge to report. For a while they stood there in silence. Then one said, "Captain, which is the Southern Cross?" His question took me by surprise. I searched the sky but couldn't find the constellation. I asked the navigator, who was familiar with such things by virtue of taking daily observations, but he said the cross wasn't showing yet, though it would appear shortly to the southeast. The pilots, saying simply, "We embark," shook hands in resolute manner and went down from the bridge.

By now Guam Island was a pitch-black mass lying straight across our path. After a little while a puff of white smoke rose up, apparently from the island. At 11 P.M. we increased to twelve knots—there was still an hour to go for the launching position. At midnight, strong impulses appeared on our radar screen, seeming to come from two different places. Was it an enemy ship or had they sighted us from shore? Anyway it looked as if their radar had picked us up. We didn't know our position accurately and it would have been fatal had we been too far off. For better or for worse I proceeded in the direction of the enemy, using my radar to check our distance from the shore. It turned out to be just seventeen miles, as planned. I prepared to dive forthwith, hoping to effect the launching before the enemy could get in an attack, but a report came from the engine room saying that water was coming in through the exhaust and that we couldn't remain submerged. There was nothing to do—we surfaced. We could still hear the enemy radar and our position was distinctly uncomfortable. In ten minutes repairs were effected and we were able to dive. While all this was going on, we were getting telephone messages from the Numbers 2 and 3 pilots who had already boarded their craft. At 2 A.M. I showed the two pilots of torpedoes Numbers 1 and 4 the lights of Guam through the periscope and, wishing them luck, gave them orders to board also. Even now the composure of the two young men remains fixed in my mind. The man whose duty it was to close the bottom flap of the torpedo finished his job and raised his hand to signal all set. At 2:30 A.M. the order was given, "Stand by to launch." Each torpedo aligned its rudder with the submarine. Until the moment of launching communication was by telephone so arranged that the connection could be ripped off when the torpedo left the parent ship.

Ten minutes later, all were ready to launch and we prepared to release the torpedoes in order. The actual time planned for launching was 3 A.M. By 4:30 A.M. it would begin to get light and by the time the torpedoes were due at their objective it would be full daylight.

Torpedo 1 reported, "All well." The last clamp was let go, her engine started, and the weapon was launched. The pilot proceeded on his way, his last contact with us, the telephone, finally severed. There she went in full cry for the enemy ships in the harbor at Guam. At the very last moment the officer pilot shouted, "Three cheers for the Emperor." Number 2 Kaiten was then launched in like manner. Despite his youth the pilot was composed to the last and went on his way without uttering a single word. Torpedo 3 was delayed till last, for too much water got into the engine, so 4 was launched third, amid more shouts of, "Three cheers for the Emperor." Finally Number 3 went off. Owing to a defect in the telephone it was impossible to have a final word with her pilot.

At that moment a loud explosion was heard which might have come from Number 3. We surfaced but all was well and we made for the open sea to escape. At

4:30 A.M. torpedo 1 was due at her target. We tried to see what was happening at Apra harbor but just at that moment an aircraft appeared and we had to dive and make off. We were not, however, attacked.

We tried to listen on the hydrophones for the sound of the torpedoes hitting their mark. After dawn we came to periscope depth and made a search to the east but it revealed only something resembling a dark cloud or smoke; nothing that could be confirmed. We remained submerged till 11 P.M. that night. At supper we prayed for the souls of the four warriors and afterward put their effects in order.

One of them, Lieutenant Ishikawa, had written the following, just before his torpedo was launched:

> The day of decisive action together with three other men on board has arrived. We are all well and in good spirits. Apra is going to be amazed. The moon is pale and the stars sparse and distant. In early January, O Miya Island (Guam), appearing to be silent in sleep, floats before me. Who knows the confusion there will be in a few hours' time? For the sake of our great country we have come to the place appointed.
>
> Only twenty-two years of life and it is now just like a dream. The meaning of life will be shown today. As the point of the decisive fight between Japan and America, just to check in one blow our decline and thus to protect for ever the illustrious three-thousand-year-old history of Great Japan.
>
> Great Japan is the land of the Gods. The land of the Gods is eternal and cannot be destroyed. Hereafter no matter, there will be thousands and tens of thousands of boys and we now offer our lives as a sacrifice for our country. Let us get away from the petty affairs of this earthly and

mundane life to the land where righteousness reigns supreme and eternal.

One of the other pilots wrote:

> Although there is always Divine Grace over our Imperial country, nevertheless without effort there is no sincerity, without righteousness and honesty there will be nothing of value. Thereafter, even if we vainly rely on the Divine Grace it will still be dangerous.
>
> Great Japan is determined to win. The decisive battle has sprung on to the enemy's territory. May the spirits of the departed in Heaven witness our fight to the bitter end.

With a feeling of anticlimax we set off on our long trip home, steering north in the direction of the Bungo Channel. It would have been in order to attack the enemy on the return journey but having stirred up the mud, I did not think there would be a chance of anything without waiting about for it. We went straightaway northward to have a look, but our routes were for the most part definitely laid down so as not to risk confusion with other submarines and it was not for me to go round searching for targets to suit my own book.

On the 14th we received the results of a photographic reconnaissance made on the 9th. There was then still one aircraft carrier at anchor and the thought that she would have left before the human torpedo threat filled me with regret. Until the 15th we only surfaced by night but had no encounters with the enemy. Orders to return were received by those submarines who had been unable to make their attack by the 14th.

On the 16th I reported by signal, "Attack carried out

according to schedule on 12th. All torpedoes launched. Results of attacks not confirmed." It was the first transmission since leaving harbor. That evening after proceeding submerged for about four hours, we heard the sound of turbines on the hydrophones. The tubes were brought to the ready. It was a pitch-dark night and there would have been nothing for it but a blind shot. At this point the sound vanished. Then we heard something different, a diesel, but this also disappeared. By January 19 we were fairly far north and it was getting cold. Just after noon we sighted a large aircraft and dived to safeguard against depth-charging, but no attack materialized. The radar just wasn't functioning.

During the night of the 20th, at the entrance to the Bungo Channel, we got an impulse on our surface radar, and while we were estimating the course, a submarine on the surface hove in sight. It was nighttime with a slight mist and bad visibility, but she looked remarkably like I-36. We made our recognition signal but there was no reply. Anyway the stranger was faster than us and soon passed out of sight. On inquiring after arrival in harbor, it turned out that it was I-36: she had had no idea of our presence.

In the meantime how had the other boats in the Kongo force fared? Submarine I-56 had made for Admiralty Island but having tried to make the approach three times, she found the enemy defenses too strong and finally returned without launching her torpedoes. Submarine I-47 penetrated safely into the Hollandia harbor entrance during daylight on the 11th. She got in while enemy patrol craft were in the midst of firing practice. She reached the launching position and launched all her torpedoes at intervals of half an hour from 4 A.M. At daylight the shore base W/T station was heard transmitting a succession of S's which was thought to indicate a submarine attack or sighting. Consequently I-47 left on her return trip with no doubts concerning the success of the attack.

Submarine I-53 went to the Kossol Passage near Palau Island but a defect prevented one torpedo from being launched and another blew up after launching owing to a burst pipe. The remaining two torpedoes were safely launched but the results were unknown.

As for I-36 it was her second operation at Ulithi. This time she approached on an opposite course, nudged a reef but was undamaged, and safely launched her torpedoes. The results, however, were not confirmed.

I-48 was due to make an attack at Ulithi on January 20, and while it was believed that she launched her torpedoes, she failed to return to harbor.

After the war we learned that I-48 was sunk in action with U. S. destroyers off Ulithi on January 22.

Altogether, the Kongo unit achieved fourteen successful launches and suffered ten failures due to various defects, and the loss of one parent submarine. As to the actual results, these are still not clear even after the war, but according to U. S. sources, I-58's attack on Guam accounted for the sinking of a large tanker, which lost most of its crew.*

---

* There are few records available to the public from either British or U. S. sources, but in the main the U.S.A. makes no specific admissions

The poor results achieved by the antiaircraft radar during these operations led to the development of an eight-section antenna. I-58's long life was in no small measure due to these improvements.

---

that any ships, either warships or merchant vessels, were sunk by this method.

It is possible that further corroboration from the above source will appear in the relevant volumes of the *History of United States Naval Operations in World War II*, by Samuel Eliot Morison, which are expected to be published in the near future.

17

ATTACKS

AT IWO JIMA

The U. S. forces began their landings on Iwo Jima on February 29, 1944. A second human-torpedo unit, the Chibaya unit, was hurriedly formed on receipt of a report that a strong U. S. fleet was bombarding the island. Submarines I-368, 370, and 44 were the parent craft. The unit sailed for Iwo Jima on February 22 and 23, but I-370 was sunk by an American destroyer off Iwo Jima on the 25th, and on the 26th, in the same area, I-368 was attacked and sunk by a U. S. carrier-borne aircraft. I-44 reached Iwo Jima, but there was sighted by an American destroyer and made to submerge for no less than forty-six and a half hours. No depth-charge attack developed, but conditions in the boat became appalling. The air contained over six per cent carbon dioxide at the end of this period. The crew were gasping like fish, and were just on the point of suffocation. In the end I-44 had to abandon the operation and return to base. The Admiral Commanding Submarines was exceedingly angry about it, and the captain was forthwith relieved of his command.

Thus the operation by the Chibaya unit ended in complete failure and in consequence another unit, Kamitake, composed of my boat, I-58, and I-36, was formed and dispatched to Iwo Jima with the intention of inflicting some damage, however small, on the enemy. We had a great send-off from Kure on March 1, 1945. Passing through the Bungo Channel, we were off Tosa by nightfall, but a depression was approaching and at daylight the next day we continued at high speed on the surface in order to avoid it. The reason for the failure of the Chibaya unit was obscure, but after much thought we planned to approach Iwo Jima from the north, the side where enemy patrols might be expected to be thin. They were very alert to the south and east of the islands, since their lines of communication crossed these areas. We should have sighted many ships and found a large number of targets in this area, but as our orders forbade us to attack shipping, for our real objective was ships at anchor, this southeastern route was unsatisfactory for the approach.

On the nights of March 3 and 4 aircraft showed up on the radar screen and in consequence we proceeded submerged. We had been equipped with the latest type of short-wave aerial and the results were excellent. As far as possible we proceeded on the surface by day as well as by night and dived at night only when visibility was bad. While submerged on the night of March 4, we heard something on the hydrophones which seemed to indicate the presence of enemy antisubmarine craft, and the same occurred on the night of the 5th for some two hours, but nothing untoward occurred. On the 5th we also picked up on a medium wave length what appeared to be telephonic communication between enemy ships engaged in bombardment. We surmised from this that the enemy was using powerful surface units for this purpose. On the 6th we were submerged by day and making the approach with great caution. At about 4 P.M. we heard the sound of four successive explosions, and at the same moment the sound of a propeller was faintly evident but soon petered out. An hour before sunset we came up to periscope depth to take a look round, and soon sighted a large warship to the south. We immediately dived, without determining her class. If she were at anchor, it would have taken an hour to approach her. By then it would have been after sunset and an attack would only have been possible in the absence of moonlight. Apart from this, the time had arrived for recharging the batteries, and had the ship been moving she would have been no target for human torpedoes.

We decided, therefore, to abandon the idea of attacking this vessel, and after charging our batteries proceeded to the most favorable area for attacking with our full complement of human torpedoes. The crew were very disgruntled at the idea of turning away from the enemy, but as we only carried Kaitens for attacking ships at anchor there was no other course of action. We were about to surface after sunset but heard the sound of propellers on the hydrophones, and as the visibility was bad we remained submerged. Before dawn on March 7 we surfaced to charge batteries. The north side of Iwo Jima was already visible on the radar screen. The sea was calm and it was a dark, moonless night. We dived before sunrise and proceeded to plot our final approach course. That same day we surfaced after sunset and made the final preparations for launching the Kaitens, and at supper that evening, according to custom, we took leave of the Kaiten crews, having explained the situation to them. It was intended to launch them early on the following morning, the 8th. Having completed charging batteries at 11 P.M., we proceeded on the surface at fifteen knots toward a position seventeen miles to the northwest of Iwo Jima, where we expected to arrive at 2 A.M. We passed through several rain squalls and the visibility was poor—excellent conditions for operating Kaitens. Enemy radar transmissions from three directions showed up on the surface radar plot, revealing the probable presence of enemy destroyers. If we were sighted, we planned to dive. The Kaitens, which had to be entered from the upper deck, were manned, and as it was still three hours until launching time, we gave them drinks to keep them going.

We had only been going for about one hour on the final approach course when we received a signal, marked urgent, reading: "Kamitake unit operation canceled—I-58 is to proceed forthwith to Okino-shima to act as wireless link ship for Combined Fleet operation to be carried out on March 11." It was maddening to be turned back right on the enemy's doorstep—I could hardly bear it. There was no question of replying by signal as that would have led immediately to our discovery. While I was weighing up the possibility of going on to launch the Kaitens before obeying the signal, a personal signal came from the Chief of Staff Combined Fleet: "Operation 'HA' is very important and your orders should be followed without fail. Report program and expected time of arrival off Okino-shima." There was nothing to do but to conform. I immediately informed the boat's crews and the Kaiten personnel. We dived during the forenoon of the 9th and in the evening we jettisoned the Kaitens and proceeded with all speed on the surface for Okino-shima. As events turned out, it was a pity that we did not attack the fine target which presented itself on the 8th. En route, we twice sighted aircraft, which kept us dived for about an hour in each case, but otherwise we proceeded on the surface at fourteen knots, eventually sighting the island according to schedule. Having completed our task, we returned to Kure in accordance with instructions. I duly reported to the C.-in-C., and, having pointed out that we could have launched our Kaitens, had another boat been detailed for this other task, I was told by one of the senior staff officers that they hadn't realized that we had got so far. What would have happened to us after launching with the enemy destroyers round about it is difficult to say, and maybe we would have failed to return, but above all I wanted to have a try! During this operation the new radar set had been accurate and reliable, but certain further trials were necessary to get absolutely foolproof results from it.

Submarine I-36 left harbor a day late and had to abandon the operation just after leaving the Bungo Channel.

18

THE BATTLE

FOR OKINAWA

On March 24 an American task force commenced the bombardment of the southeast coast of Okinawa, and our submarines were ordered to concentrate there with all speed. Submarines I-8, RO-46, and 41 proceeded to this area to search for the enemy, but all were lost. The enemy were able to mount overwhelming antisubmarine operations, for they had complete control by sea and in the air. However, the Tatara unit was formed, comprising submarines I-47, 56, 58, and 44, each carrying six redesigned Kaitens. I-47 left the base for Okinawa on March 29. She passed through the Bungo Channel safely, but just off Miyazaki she was suddenly attacked by over fifty small aircraft which she had thought to be friendly. The boat crash-dived and got away. Some thirty bombs were dropped, but there was no damage and the boat was able to surface and continue on her southward journey about an hour later. At about 2:30 A.M. the next morning two warships were sighted about six thousand yards to the south. The lookout reported them as cruisers and the boat dived preparatory to attack. A closer inspection by periscope, however, revealed destroyers. It was too late to do anything about it, and four hours later the submarine was attacked with depth charges but eventually got away from the enemy just off Tanega Island. She surfaced after sunset and was busy trying to investigate an oil leakage from the main tanks when more aircraft suddenly attacked. A near miss, just after she crash-dived, caused the oil leaks to get worse, so she turned back for Kure.

Two other submarines, I-56 and 44, set out on April 3, but nothing more was ever heard of them. After the war we heard that both were sunk off Okinawa by American destroyers. We ourselves in I-58 left the base on April 2 with the same Kaiten crews we had carried in our frustrated operation against Iwo Jima. The operational plan was flexible, depending on the enemy's disposition. I had made a point of asking H.Q. to send me detailed reports of enemy dispositions off Okinawa, particulars of their destroyer patrols off the northern side of the island. As usual, we passed through the Bungo Channel during darkness, keeping a very strict antisubmarine lookout. The following day, April 2, we dived during daylight hours and continued on our southward run. There were heavy clouds during the night and visibility was bad. We had to take avoiding action for aircraft on both April 2 and 3, but nothing untoward occurred, and we arrived safely off Yaku Island. We decided provisionally to approach from the west, but in the event of the enemy's having already formally occupied Chujo Bay, there was a possibility that the eastern approach might be safer. However, we finally decided to come in from the west, for this gave a better chance of catching the enemy task forces and transports at anchor, when they would present the best target for the Kaitens. Thus, in the dead of night on April 3, we made our way in. We sighted what appeared to be a submarine on the surface near the center of the channel and immediately dived, but lost contact after about an hour, surfaced again and continued on our way on a zigzag course. At daylight the next day we had to dive again, for our radar indicated an aircraft. This happened not less than seven times in all on the 5th and 6th; we had no means of telling whether the aircraft was friend or foe. This put us behind schedule, and it wasn't until the 6th that we reached the area to the west of Amami Oshima. At about 1 P.M. we sighted a mast on the horizon, dived, and confirmed it to be a small antisubmarine vessel—whether friend or foe we couldn't be certain, but from all appearances it seemed to be an enemy. As the battle area neared Japanese waters, it was easy to be careless and mistakenly assume all vessels—and aircraft for that matter—to be Japanese.

The weather began to deteriorate with low, dark clouds and rough sea, and we began to worry as to whether the Kaitens could be launched. However, we hoped for calmer weather in Okinawa anchorage. Our course to Okinawa was well out to sea, and it was therefore difficult to get an accurate position in the prevailing bad weather. We couldn't even pick up the island by radar, and, being harassed by aircraft both by day and night, we had insufficient time for charging batteries. In fact the appearance of even one destroyer might have been the end of us. By the 7th conditions had not improved, and we had little time on the surface. We still had only our estimated position to rely on. To make matters worse, there was also the set of two knots caused by the Japan current. The same day, the 7th, we had word that we were to be joined by the battleship *Yamato* and thought that we should be making the Okinawa attack in company. In fact, the *Yamato* had been sunk.

On the 8th a signal was received from the C.-in-C. Combined Fleet to go in and fight to the death, and we surfaced, fully resolved to make direct for our objective. Later that day we ran into a large patrol aircraft of the type used on antisubmarine sweeping operations. Almost giving up hope, we crash-dived, but to our surprise no bombs fell. Nevertheless we had to continue submerged during daylight, and as air patrols continued by night we were unable to charge our batteries. Had this continued we would have been powerless to deliver even one attack. We thought of coming up for a short spell, doing a quick charge, and then waiting for the weather to moderate before trying a second time. In the end we turned back to near Kyushu. When we checked our position we found we were forty-five miles out. We made some essential repairs to the Kaitens and then turned toward Okinawa for another try, but the weather was still as bad as ever, and we were harassed by aircraft both by day and by night. There was no respite for charging, and it seemed that we would be faced with the same difficulties as before.

On the 14th we suddenly had orders to stand out into the Pacific. First we had to cross one of our own mine fields, thence to the Chinese mainland, and finally out into the Pacific by the coast of Formosa. We had expended no less than seven days in trying to make the approach for an attack on Okinawa, but the attempt was of no avail in the prevailing conditions. We were attacked by aircraft over fifty times and the longest time we were able to remain surfaced was just under four hours. During the two days when we were nearest Okinawa the longest period was one hour and ten minutes. Our radar, too, must have been unreliable, as we would sometimes suffer an air attack two minutes after surfacing. Submarine batteries normally require four to five hours for charging and six hours for topping up fully. One charging of the air compressor will provide sufficient high-pressure air for surfacing three or four times, and it takes about half an hour to charge the air cylinders fully. Under the difficult conditions we had experienced it would have been possible, with careless handling, to run completely out of high-pressure air for surfacing, quite apart from the matter of battery charging. One destroyer in the offing, keeping the boat under for a whole day, would have caused the half-charged batteries to peter out, making submerged movement impossible. Then again, submarines carrying Kaitens had no guns, so that it was equally impracticable to surface in haste to fight it out, as our sole armament consisted of two machine guns. Kaitens could be used in good weather, but their use was quite impracticable in the stormy conditions prevailing at that time. This seemed particularly galling, for we hadn't met a single destroyer, nor had we been sighted. Owing to the efficiency of our antiaircraft radar, we came through without being bombed—a change indeed from the situation six months earlier.

We emerged into the Pacific from the direction of the east coast of Formosa, and proceeded on a northerly course at a distance of some three to four hundred miles from Okinawa, but met no enemy surface forces and only an occasional aircraft. At about 1 A.M. on April 25 we were proceeding on the surface in a calm sea with a slight swell when we got an enemy radar contact on surface radar. We at once dived to await the outcome. Soon we sighted through the periscope a ship burning navigation lights. It turned out to be a hospital ship and we let it go by. At about 3 A.M. came the sound of nine successive explosions. We were keeping both a periscope and hydrophone watch and sighted a group of one or two masts as we rose and fell in the swell. There were three ships. At first we identified them as cruisers, but as they appeared more clearly they looked more like small destroyers. As we steadily studied the situation the ships hoisted a string of flags and turned toward us. Had we been sighted? The Kaitens were inoperable as over a month had elapsed since leaving the base, and they had had no maintenance. There was nothing for it but to escape. We dived deep to two hundred and seventy feet. All was silent throughout the boat. After about half an hour we heard the sound of propellers of three ships. So they had found us at last. All we could do was to remain still. In the boat we were at depth-charge defense stations. The sound of propellers grew louder. One passed from astern to right overhead, the others on either side. We were all set for the attack. Everything was dead quiet inside the boat and the tension was almost unbearable. To our surprise and relief, however, they passed right over us and away. There was the sound of the explosion of one depth charge, but by that time they were well clear. The enemy was clearly not the man we thought him! We altered course away from the direction of the explosion and made our escape. We might have got clear away from the enemy, but we thought we were on a line of communication. Unfortunately, the order to return to base came and we made our way north, arriving in port on April 29. While on passage an enemy mine exploded close by, bringing to the surface a large number of fish which helped us to celebrate the Emperor's birthday in proper fashion.

On arrival at Kure we found that none of the submarines which had gone to Okinawa had returned. Submarine RO-109 reported having been attacked with three hundred depth charges and had been recalled, but she failed to return, and in fact I-58 was the only boat to return safely from the operation. A conference was held to discuss the operation as it concerned I-58 and RO-109. As a result it was decided that it was futile to try to penetrate the invasion routes on strongly defended bases and that all we could do was to attack the enemy's lines of communication. The Okinawa campaign wasn't the first occasion on which this same problem had cropped up, but now we only had four large submarines left, and it was decided to equip the I-300 transport submarine for carrying Kaitens.

After the war we heard that the other submarines taking part in the Okinawa campaign had all been sunk in action with U. S. destroyers to the east and southeast of Okinawa Island. A survivor from I-8, one of the first submarines to receive instructions to proceed to Okinawa, related his experiences as follows:

> At about 10:30 P.M. on March 30 the lookout sighted an approaching enemy destroyer and I-8 immediately crash-dived and received her first depth-charge attack at a depth of about ninety feet. She was then continuously attacked for four hours until she eventually sank. The attacks were accurate, as the enemy was easily able to determine our position by the sound of our propellers. As the attacks increased in intensity, the crew's quarters aft were holed and the compartment started to flood. We did our best to effect repairs, but it was of little avail, and the boat went down to four hundred and fifty feet, with the bow inclining upward at an angle of twenty-five degrees, causing

the bilge water to surge aft. The boat continued to sink. Something had to be done and the captain gave the order to blow the after-tanks. This made bubbles rise to the surface, causing a white patch which provided an excellent target for the attackers. We stood by awaiting death. All our torpedoes were gone and the captain decided to surface and try to fight it out with the gun. Orders were given to blow the main ballast tanks. All power in the boat was already stopped. It was 2 A.M. on March 31. I was one of the gun's crew, standing by in the conning tower while the boat surfaced at an angle of twenty degrees. The hatches were opened and we emerged. There was a destroyer to starboard and we engaged with the 25-mm. machine gun. Two of us manned the 14-cm. gun and had just got it loaded when I was wounded in the foot by a shell splinter. I tried to get on to the bridge but at that moment it was blown apart, leaving a large gaping hole. I was just trying to get back to the gun when I sighted an enemy cruiser. Attacked by two enemy warships at a range of about three thousand yards, I-8 hadn't the slightest chance. Soon she turned over and sank. It was by this time 2:30 A.M. I was in great pain but managed to keep afloat. There was one other person floating, but I didn't know who it was. There was plenty of wind with a big swell and pale moonlight. After what seemed like about two hours I came to in the sick bay of the U. S. destroyer.

19

THE SEARCH

FOR THE

ENEMY

Of the special Kaiten unit which carried out attacks at Iwo Jima, two out of five submarines failed to return, and at Okinawa two out of four met the same fate. Those which safely returned had been unable to launch any Kaitens. In fact this form of attack was quite ineffective against strongly defended anchorages. However, it became of paramount importance to attack ships under way, and submarines carrying Kaitens were so adapted that the crews of the Kaitens could all embark from the inside of the boat while submerged. The submarines were also adapted to carry an increased number of Kaitens. Two submarines, I-47 and 36, forming the Amatake unit, left the base on April 12 and 20 respectively to carry out the first of these operations against ships under way. Eight of the twelve Kaitens carried were launched and each of them accounted for a transport or a destroyer. When attacking ships under way, two or three practice runs were inadequate and six practice launches from the parent submarine became standard drill.

On May 5, I-367 left the base and, with two of her five Kaitens, succeeded in sinking two unspecified ships to the east of Okinawa.

Between May 23 and June 15, I-361 patrolled in the Okinawa area but failed to return. I-363, ordered to attack the Okinawa-Ulithi line of communication, failed to find any targets and returned without launching any Kaitens. I-165 went to the Marianas but failed to return.

I-36, after a grueling patrol, was lucky enough to survive. This boat left the base on June 6 for the Marianas area. On the voyage she found all her Kaitens to be defective. She succeeded in repairing three of the six. Off Saipan she sighted a merchant ship and launched a Kaiten, but the merchant ship was on the alert and made her escape. I-36 pursued her for an hour and a half, when suddenly she sighted a destroyer through the periscope at a range of a thousand yards. The periscope was hurriedly lowered, but too late—two depth charges came crashing down, putting the rudder out of action. Half an hour later the destroyer returned to the area and continued her attacks, passing over the boat four times. It was too much! The Kaiten crews asked to be released and orders were given for launching, but the electrically operated steering gear of the Kaitens wouldn't function and telephone communications with the inside of the boat were cut. Launching orders were canceled, but by this time a second destroyer appeared and joined in the attack. As this increased the risk of making the Kaitens completely useless, two were launched. Twenty minutes later there was a loud explosion as more depth charges were fired. I-36 dived deep to escape these attacks and after two days of great discomfort she eventually surfaced in a spot clear of the enemy. Her batteries were all but run down and there was only sufficient high-pressure air to surface once more. Nevertheless, I-36 managed to limp back to Kure on June 30.

In 1942 it was decided to build eighteen large submarines, each capable of carrying three torpedo bombers, and it was rumored that the trial planes to be used were nearing completion. However, while waiting for these craft to be completed, the war situation continued to deteriorate. In December, 1944, I-400, the first of the class, was completed, to be followed by I-401 in January, 1945. In addition to these, submarines I-13 and 14, converted to flagship submarines and carrying two aircraft, were completed by January and the end of February, 1945, respectively.

These four boats were formed into one unit under the command of Captain Arizumi and commenced their trials in the Inland Sea. The objective was the bombing of the Panama Canal. However, the aircraft designed for us in this operation were not yet complete; two only had carried out trials and no training with the parent submarine was possible.

At the end of April, 1945, combined training with the aircraft was carried out in the Sea of Japan. Meanwhile there had been various mishaps—I-401 had grazed a mine and the departure of the unit had to be postponed, but the planning of the operation was gradually taking shape.

The I-400 class had a cruising radius of forty thousand miles and would still have some fuel remaining after a return journey to Panama. The converted I-13 had insufficient cruising radius and she was to have fueled from 1-400 en route. Both types were to have carried provisions for four months. In all, ten aircraft were due to be used, six with torpedoes and four with bombs, and it was planned to make two strikes on the locks in one particular spot and completely destroy them. Models of the locks were made and many tests carried out. At the end of June combined training was carried out with each aircraft but of these two crashed and were destroyed.

In the meantime the situation continued to get worse and the heavy U. S. air attacks on Japan proper were thought to presage a landing. Submarine I-122 was attacked by a U. S. submarine in the Sea of Japan and very soon it was impossible to find any safe training area. In these circumstances this was no time for operating against the far-distant Panama Canal. Since there was a pressing need to attack the aircraft carriers at anchor on Ulithi in the Mandated Area, it was decided that I-14 and 13, each carrying two Ayagumos, the latest type of reconnaissance plane, should proceed to Truk for an air reconnaissance of Ulithi. They sailed from Ominato on July 15, but I-13 was sunk early the next day by a U. S. carrier-borne plane. I-14 arrived safely at Truk, subsequently followed by I-400 and 401. The plan for the attack on Panama had not been entirely discarded and it was intended that submarines I-400 and 401 should carry out a dawn attack on Ulithi and then proceed to Panama, after recovering their aircraft. The attack on Ulithi was planned for August 25, the submarines leaving Truk at the beginning of that month.

On August 16 came the end of the war. Nothing was ever achieved by these three-thousand-five-hundred-ton craft. They were the largest of their kind in the world. Three and a half years of planning and design in vain! Captain Arizumi, the senior officer, shot himself just before their arrival in Yokosuka at the end of August.

In 1946 both I-400 and I-401 were taken to the U.S.A. by the U. S. naval authorities. The third ship of the class, I-402, was completed immediately before the war ended, but she had been converted during building to a fuel carrier.

20

THE SINKING

OF THE

INDIANAPOLIS

In July, 1945, I-58 was ready again for active service. We were ordered to leave Kure on the 16th to harass the enemy's communications. We left harbor to the strains of martial music amid a host of cheering voices and set course through the swept channel. We spent one night off the Kaiten base and held a special ceremony to mark the coming ordeal of the Kaiten crews. There were six of these brave men on board. The next morning we proceeded to sea, escorted out by a score of motor boats. We carried out deep-diving trials at the entrance to the Bungo Channel, but the periscopes of the Kaitens were found to be defective and we had to return to base to change them. However, we got away again on the evening of the 18th and proceeded southward through the Bungo Channel, zigzagging at high speed for fear of enemy submarines.

A submarine on the surface has no means of dealing with a submerged enemy, and all she can do is to make a dash for it on the surface, hoping no enemy aircraft appear. Provided the submarine is equipped with air and surface radar, as she goes along she can pick up the enemy's outline on the surface, obtain his position and course and so take avoiding action. At daybreak enemy submarines were likely to dive, and so did we, resulting in a stalemate. At night both boats will surface and repeat the same cat-and-mouse performance. In this manner it is possible to negotiate with safety waters where enemy submarines may be lurking. At times therefore we were able to proceed at high speed on the surface toward the enemy lines of communication. That night we picked up on our radar something that appeared to be a B-29 formation, probably going to attack the Japanese mainland. One wondered what city was in for it that night. The moon was growing brighter and we had already reached the area on the Saipan-Okinawa route where we might expect to fall in with the enemy. As usual we toasted the Kaitens' crews at the evening meal. I explained the general situation to them. Our orders were to attack enemy ships off the east coast of the Philippine Islands.

I-53 had sailed with us; she was to patrol the area east of Okinawa. There was nothing to be seen except a wide expanse of ocean. We decided to lie in wait at the point where the enemy routes from their major bases at Leyte, Saipan, Okinawa, Guam, Palau, and Ulithi converged, but we fully realized that even so we might miss our chance in such a wide area. However, we had the Kaitens and were determined to sink any boat that came our way. We arrived on the Okinawa-Saipan route, but still there were no signs of the enemy. The sea was calm under a bright moon; conditions were excellent but not a single target came our way.

We had no better luck on the Okinawa-Guam route. It was then full moon on the 22nd; with conditions suitable for attack by day or by night we proceeded at speed to the Leyte-Guam route. The moon was waning and our best chance was fading away. I went to pray at the ship's shrine.

On July 27, in accordance with instructions, we arrived on the Guam-Leyte route and made along it to the west. At 5:30 A.M. on the 28th, an enemy aircraft showed up on the radar and at once we dived. By this time our radar equipment had improved and we no longer had to worry about being surprised by enemy aircraft.

At 2 P.M. we came up to periscope depth and to my great joy inspection revealed a slowly approaching, three-masted ship. It was a large tanker. At last we were face to face with the elusive enemy. The enemy appeared to be unaware of our presence. As we watched a destroyer came into sight—this made the situation less simple. As we dived to creep in closer I gave the order, "Kaitens prepare for action"; "All tubes to the ready." Our hydrophones were not functioning well, making it unwise to approach to within torpedo range, because we couldn't be sure of the destroyer's whereabouts, so I decided to use the Kaitens. "Numbers one and two Kaitens—Stand by!" Number 1 was a little slow and I decided to launch Number 2 first. I gave them the enemy course and speed by telephone. At 2:31 P.M. Number 2 Kaiten started her engines and reported ready. I gave the order to launch 2. The last securing band was slipped and she set off on her way toward the enemy tanker. Ten minutes later 1 was ready. Her officer shouted, "Three cheers for the Emperor," and was off. Both Kaitens seemed to be running well. There were the usual South Sea squalls about, but we could still see the target quite well. But no explosion was forthcoming. Anxiously we kept watch through the periscope. Finally the tanker disappeared from view. About fifty minutes after the launch of Number 2 Kaiten the sound of an explosion was reported and ten minutes later another one. We surfaced but a squall obscured everything. Our thoughts were with the men who had so recently been with us— and we prayed for their happiness in a future existence.

It was our tenth day out from Kure and our supply of fresh vegetables had given out. There were a few onions still left but otherwise it was just tinned food from morning till night. Our tinned vegetables were particularly unpopular—except for a kind of parsley. There were also plenty of tinned sweet potatoes; they were generally held to taste of sand or ashes.

Continuing our patrol, we made off for the intersection of the Leyte-Guam and Palau-Okinawa routes. July 29 was cloudy and the weather mostly bad, but it wasn't rough and we continued on the surface toward our objective. We had complete confidence in our four large binoculars and air and surface radar, and were firmly convinced that we would spot the enemy before he spotted us. We were apprehensive only of enemy submarines in good visibility but otherwise we were confident that we would not be exposed to an unexpected attack. Both crew and armament were first class. If only our submarines had had radar two years earlier, we should not have incurred so many losses and would have had more submarines for current use.

I thought I would continue on the surface but toward nightfall the visibility deteriorated and by about 7 P.M. it was almost nil. We decided to wait for the visibility to improve and dived to await moonrise at 10 P.M. After diving, the chief engineer came to inquire how soon we should be surfacing again—he was anxious to make minor repairs which had been impossible to tackle while he had been running on the surface almost continuously. He was glad to have the opportunity of two hours' work before moonrise. I raised the periscope to check what was happening but it was pitch black and I could see nothing.

Leaving orders to be called at 10:30 P.M. I went to lie down on my bunk in the wardroom. The vessel was moving slowly westward at a submerged speed of two knots with an underwater displacement of three thousand tons. All was silent in the dimly lighted boat except for the sound of the air-conditioning plant and the characteristic sound of the hydroplanes and rudder movements. Two thirds of the crew were turned in. They slept completely naked on top of the torpedoes, on top of the rice sacks, or between shelves. The boat was a modern one and the cooling plant therefore pretty good. The remaining third of the crew were on watch, with the engine-room staff carrying out minor repairs. One must not forget the rats, of which there were plenty! They were a perfect plague and it was impossible to keep them down. At the moment they were scampering about the kitchen and making an awful row. At 10:30 P.M. the petty officer of the watch came to call me, reporting all well. I donned my uniform and having paid a visit to the boat's shrine, mounted the conning tower. The officer of the watch had nothing to report and, wishing to raise the periscope to have a look round, I ordered, "Night action stations." By then it was 11 P.M. and about an hour after moonrise. My eyes became accustomed to the darkness. I ordered, "Sixty feet," and increased speed to three knots. When we came up to the correct depth, I ordered the night periscope to be raised just clear of the surface and quickly took a look round. The visibility was much better and one could almost see the horizon. The moon was already high in the eastern sky and there were few clouds in its vicinity. It was nearly half-moon and the light good enough for a submerged attack. Raising the periscope gradually till it was well above the surface, I made a careful search two or three times but there was nothing in sight and I decided to surface. I ordered, "Stand by type-thirteen radar"—this was our search set for aircraft. Then I ordered, "Stand by type-twenty-two radar"—our surface radar. The receiver rose above the surface but there was no aircraft reaction. The radar operator had gone through special training and his technical skill was far above the average. Having decided that there were no enemy aircraft about, we surfaced to look for the enemy and I ordered, "Action stations." The alarm bells rang and the crew came running up to their stations. The boat suddenly became a hive of activity and in a minute or so came the report, "Crew closed up at action stations." Having housed the periscope handles, I gave the order, "Surface" and, "Blow main ballast." High-pressure air was admitted to the main tanks— the water was expelled and the boat quickly rose to the surface. As soon as the upper deck was awash, the order was given to open the conning-tower hatch and the yeoman of signals who was standing by opened up and climbed onto the bridge. He was followed by the navigator. I myself was watching through the night periscope. The surface radar set was ready to go into action. When fresh air began to come in, we changed to the low-pressure air pump for expelling the water, in order to conserve high-pressure air. At that moment the navigator shouted, "Bearing red nine-zero degrees, a possible enemy ship." I lowered the periscope, made for the bridge, and turned my binoculars in the direction indicated by the navigator. Without doubt there was a black spot which was clearly visible on the horizon on the rays of the moon. I ordered, "Dive." At this order the four people on the bridge scrambled down the ladder, the signalman last, shutting the hatch and reporting it closed. I was at the periscope in which the black shape was clear. I ordered, "Open the vents," the water came into the tanks and the boat started to go down. I kept my eye glued to the periscope so as not to lose sight of the target. The boat was soon fully submerged. The whole operation was so much part of our life that it went as smoothly as a reflex action.

As soon as we were fully submerged I gave the orders: "Ship in sight," "All tubes to the ready," "Kaitens stand by." It was 11:08 P.M. After diving we had altered course to port and the black shape was now right ahead. I was still watching through the periscope, from time to time scanning the rest of the field of view, but there was nothing else in sight. Gradually the supposed enemy seemed to be getting closer. We were ready to give a salvo of six torpedoes. The dark shape continued on a course which was bringing it straight toward us. Was it a destroyer coming on for a depth-charge attack, having already detected our existence? Even if it was not, it would be difficult to score a torpedo hit if it came straight on over the top of us. I had some bad moments when thinking it might be a destroyer. In the darkness of the conning tower, it was impossible to tell the color of the people's faces and if the others detected that the captain was feeling uneasy, they could only surmise this from his voice. We couldn't estimate the range since we didn't know the class of ship. We couldn't yet hear anything on the hydrophones. .The round black spot gradually became triangular in shape. The time was 11:09 P.M. "Six torpedoes will be fired." I decided to fire from all tubes in one salvo. At the same time I ordered the crew of Kaiten 6 to embark and Number 5 to stand by.

The triangular shape gradually got bigger. It was still making straight for us. At this rate it would pass right over us. It was difficult to estimate the range as we couldn't see the height of the mast. It was necessary to know range, course, and speed of the target in order to aim and obtain a hit—for the most part the captain at the periscope had to make the necessary estimate. In the case of a merchant ship one could get the course and speed by following up astern, obtaining the range by radar, but using it meant chancing giving away one's position to the enemy before firing, and it was difficult to know when to use it. If the class of ship were known, its speed, of course, could be deduced by counting the engine revolutions with the hydrophones. Anyway, many possible errors were involved, and in order to insure a hit, the error had to be kept as small as possible and the salvo of six torpedoes had to be fired fanwise. As there were changes in course and speed, the time of firing had to be determined in advance, and this was especially difficult at night. It was possible, however, in conditions of not less than half-moon.

The target began to assume the appearance of a large warship, and the uppermost part of the triangular black spot had resolved itself into two portions. There was a large mast forward. We've got her, I thought. The fact that the enemy was now visible in two distinct portions made it less likely that she would pass right over us, and the class of ship was now apparent. I was able to assess the masthead height as ninety feet. She was either a battleship or large cruiser. The range fell to four thousand yards. The expected range at time of firing—two thousand yards—and the bearing—green forty-five degrees—were set. A hydrophone report gave the enemy speed as moderately high. I used this estimate for the moment, but visual observation didn't put it so high, and I altered the setting to twenty knots. As for the Kaitens, I had been so occupied with the ordinary torpedoes that I hadn't given the orders for standing by to launch though the Kaiten crews kept coming to ask about it. A Kaiten attack at this stage of the moon would be difficult and I determined not to use them unless the ordinary torpedo attack failed.

We had the moon behind us and the enemy ship was now clearly visible. She had two turrets aft and a large tower mast. I took her to be an *Idaho*-class battleship. The crew were all agog, awaiting the order to fire the torpedoes. All was dead quiet. In such circumstances the eyes of the boat were in the captain's head, and the hydrophones supplied the ears. Without him the crew could know nothing of what was going on outside. They waited tensely for the next order. Questions kept coming from the Kaiten crews: "What about the enemy?" "Where's the enemy?" "Why can't we be launched?" The favorable moment for firing was approaching. I altered the setting of the director to green sixty degrees, range fifteen hundred yards, and began the approach for firing. At last, in a loud voice, I gave the order, "Stand by—Fire!" The torpedo-release switch pressed at intervals of two seconds and then the report came from the torpedo room, "All tubes fired and correct." Six torpedoes were speeding, fanwise, toward the enemy ship. I took a quick look through the periscope, but there was nothing else in sight. Bringing the boat on to a course parallel with the enemy, we waited anxiously. Every minute seemed an age. Then on the starboard side of the enemy by the forward turret, and then by the after turret there rose columns of water, to be followed immediately by flashes of bright red flame. Then another column of water rose from alongside Number 2 turret and seemed to envelop the whole ship—"A hit, a hit!" I shouted as each torpedo struck home, and the crew danced round with joy. There was still nothing else in sight and the enemy was stopped but still afloat. I raised the day periscope and gave the conning-tower crew a sight. Soon came the sound of a heavy explosion, far greater than that of the actual hits. Three more heavy explosions followed in quick succession, then six more. The crew, not realizing the cause, were shouting, "Depth-charge attack," so I hastily reassured them that it was our target exploding and that there was no other enemy in sight. I saw several flashes aboard the enemy, but she showed no signs of sinking. I therefore stood by to give her a second salvo. From the Kaitens came the cry, "Since the enemy won't sink, send us." The enemy certainly presented an easy target for them in spite of the dark, but what if she should sink before the Kaitens reached her? Once launched they were gone for good, and it seemed a pity to risk wasting them. I therefore decided not to use them this time. I intended to take my time, but a report came that the enemy was using her underwater detector apparatus—no doubt trying to get our range. Realizing that the enemy would get a good contact, I decided to dive deep while reloading for the second salvo, and I lowered the periscope, relying on the hydrophones and underwater detector apparatus for keeping track of the enemy. In actual fact we heard after the war that she was just on the point of sinking, but at the time this was still in doubt. We had certainly scored hits with three torpedoes, but these had so far failed to sink her. Next another report came that the sound of the detector apparatus had ceased. As we were reloading there was a list on the boat, and it would be dangerous to rise to periscope depth. As soon as reloading was completed, we surfaced and raised periscope only to find there was nothing to be seen. I made for the spot where I thought she would have sunk, but still couldn't see anything. However, it was over an hour since the first action and I was certain now that she had sunk. A ship so damaged could not have got away at high speed. Even had she got away she would still have been in sight. I wanted, however, some proof that she had definitely sunk, but it was difficult to spot any flotsam in the darkness. With feelings of regret I made off to the northeast for fear of reprisals from ships or aircraft which might have been in company with our late enemy, and after running on the surface for an hour we dived to prepare for the next encounter. The ship we had sunk turned out to be the *Indianapolis*.

We got no further opportunities for some time, and while the morale of the crew was good, despite the many hardships, the Kaiten crews couldn't be pacified. One of them was very resentful. He demanded, with tears in his eyes, why the Kaitens couldn't have been used for a good target like a battleship. So I tried to calm him down by saying that there would soon be another good target. At length, on the 30th, we celebrated our haul of the previous day with our favorite rice with beans, boiled eels, and corned beef (all of it tinned).

On August 1 we were ordered by signal to take a northerly direction, and altered course accordingly. Thinking that they would be good hunting grounds for shipping, I decided to investigate conditions on the Okinawa-Ulithi and then Okinawa-Leyte routes. At noon that day we submerged and lay in wait for the enemy, but there was nothing doing, so we surfaced at 3 P.M. and went farther north. We used the sound apparatus with meticulous care and searched frequently with the periscope, but nothing came in sight. We had surfaced and were making northward at twelve knots on the surface when we sighted a mast on the horizon. A look through the periscope revealed the hull, bridge, and funnels of a ship which I estimated to be of eight or ten thousand tons. It was a westbound unescorted merchant ship. The range was twenty thousand yards and we were slightly before her starboard beam. We increased speed to fifteen knots, but the range gradually increased. Though we increased to full speed we were unable to get ahead of the fast enemy ship. I-58 had been fitted with small engines, the double-acting diesels with which the rest of the class was equipped having been turned down on the score of production difficulties. Ballast made up for loss of weight. How we bemoaned the deficiency in Japan's industrial resources. I recalled the speed of twenty-three knots at which submarine I-24 had cruised in the Hawaiian area. The moon was on the wane, so even if we came up with the enemy there would be no hope of getting in an attack at nighttime. If possible, therefore, the enemy had to be captured by day. On the 2nd we had a radio intelligence report from the Yawata Communications Unit: "Heavy enemy W/T traffic indicating large enemy warships searching for wreck." It was by then some three days or more since we had sunk the *Indianapolis*, and we didn't realize that these signals were in fact concerned with her. We learned after the war that the captain and three hundred and fifteen of the crew had been rescued. At the time I thought it probable that rescue would be effected, for they had had ample time to radio their consorts before the ship actually sank.

It was, I think, August 7 when we received a press report announcing the great damage at Hiroshima by only one bomb. The diving officer, Submarine-lieutenant Nishimura, who normally listened in to the American news, pointed out that these could be no ordinary bombs, but I made no attempt to listen to him, nor did I want to do so, for it was lowering to morale. We on board were in no position to assess the situation. Our job was to continue the fight according to our orders and do our utmost to inflict damage on the enemy. Had I listened to the foreign broadcasts, I would probably have realized that it was the atom bomb. In about March, 1944, Dr. Tanaka had announced the existence of the bomb in the Diet, and since then we had been dreaming of the possibility of achieving it as the one means of recovery. Had we known that the enemy had already developed this weapon, our morale would have sunk and the will to fight would have evaporated. It was probably better that we remained in ignorance. From another point of view it is very dangerous to fight without knowing about new enemy weapons and their capabilities. In other words, it was necessary for senior officers only to listen to enemy broadcasts, and for them to be stouthearted enough not to let such news worry them. Unfortunately my nerves were not capable of standing the strain. Apparently when the B-29 took off from Tenian (in the Marshalls) with the atom bomb for Hiroshima, the crew had heard about the sinking of the *Indianapolis*, which had brought a portion of the bomb from the U.S.A. to Tenian, and they wrote on the side of the bomb, "A present for the souls of the *Indianapolis* crew." This story I found in March, 1949, in a magazine article entitled "The Atom Bomb Unit—to a point over Hiroshima." The atom bomb was said to have several components. Most of these were transported by aircraft, but the large and heavy section was transported by the *Indianapolis*.

It was over twenty days since we had put out from Kure and we were all pretty dirty. We had few changes of even summer clothing and we wore the same things day and night. There was no water with which to do any laundry, and in any case there was no place to dry the clothes. If they weren't properly dried the dampness inside the boat made them very sticky, and this was dangerous with a lot of electrical gear about.

THE KAITENS'

FINAL BATTLE

After sinking the *Indianapolis,* which we had thought to be an *Idaho*-class battleship, I-58 made her way north. On August 9 an atom bomb similar to the one dropped at Hiroshima was dropped at Nagasaki. The damage suffered by the Japanese mainland was becoming rapidly and progressively worse. It was reported, too, that the

Soviet Union had joined in the fight against Japan. The determination was still there, but there was little we could do. However, the morale on board I-58 was very good.

While submerged during the forenoon of August 10, our sound detector picked up an echo. I raised the periscope and found there was a destroyer some way off. I ordered the crews of 5 and 6 Kaitens to stand by. The range was about seven thousand yards and the enemy was zigzagging. There was a hitch in getting 6 launched as she was running "cold" and sending up foaming white bubbles. The sea was calm and there was a risk of being sighted by the destroyer if we hung about under these conditions, so I gave the order to stop the engine. This took some time. When I looked through the periscope the foam had not dispersed—it was giving away our position. The Kaitens' engines were making a rattling sound and I was sure we had been sighted. As I waited impatiently, the engine suddenly stopped. I didn't raise the periscope, expecting a depth-charge attack. When moments passed and no attack developed, I decided to take a look, and, to my surprise, the destroyer was now farther off. Her nearest position had been about five thousand yards, but no doubt in the excitement I had failed to notice that she had moved away. In fact, since the advent of Kaitens, enemy destroyers had not been quite so confident as before. In the meantime the captains of 3 and 4 Kaitens had embarked. Number 3 was found to be defective. So far only 5 had been launched; she was making toward the destroyer. As another destroyer and a convoy now put in an appearance, 4 was launched. She penetrated the convoy right in front of the destroyer, and with the sound of the explosion the whole convoy was thrown into confusion. On hearing the sound of another explosion, I looked through the periscope to see that the first destroyer had disappeared, indicating that she, too, had been sunk. Having prayed for our departed warriors, we surfaced and made off to the north.

That night, while we were dived, avoiding enemy aircraft, we picked up a sound on the detector apparatus. It was a pitch-black night. It was probably a merchant ship, as the sound was that of a piston engine. The Kaitens had been warned to stand by, but it was too dark to use them. Next we picked up the sound of a destroyer quite close. According to the hydrophones, the merchant ship was a big one, but owing to the darkness we could do nothing. If only there had been a moon! The sound of the approaching destroyer became louder. I determined to turn toward it and lie quiet. The enemy seemed to be turning to starboard, and we followed round toward him, standing by for a depth-charge attack. Then the sound was audible all round us and it seemed he may have found us. Perhaps he was passing over the top of us. All was dead silent within the boat as we waited. However, nothing transpired and the crisis was over.

On August 12 the sea was calm. As we made our way northward on the surface at twelve knots, we picked up enemy radar contact which appeared to be surface radar. We were increasing speed, intending to get ahead of the enemy, when another contact showed up from the same direction. After about a quarter of an hour we sighted a mast and crash-dived. It was 5:16 P.M. when I sighted the enemy, and I gave the order for the Kaitens and the torpedo tubes' crews to stand by. The target was getting nearer, and I ordered, "Number three Kaiten crew embark and stand by for launching." At 5:47 P.M. I identified the enemy as a fifteen-thousand-ton seaplane carrier. The Kaitens were all set. At 5:56 P.M. I gave the order to start up the motors. Two minutes later Number 3 Kaiten was making for the enemy: his chance had come at last. When I had another look after the launching, there was one destroyer ahead of the target. A little later the merchant ship was still there, and as I wondered what had happened I could see black smoke belching from the ship's funnels. The enemy, having sighted the Kaiten, was making off with all speed. I could see her zigzagging as she gathered speed. Half an hour passed, then came the sound of an explosion—perhaps a hit? But ten more explosions followed. Clearly the destroyer had turned about and was making a depth-charge attack. I was very anxious—my hands were clammy with sweat. At 6:42 P.M. a large column of water accompanied by volumes of black smoke were seen rising skyward. I unconsciously offered up a prayer. After an instant there was the sound of a single explosion. When the column of water had subsided and the smoke cleared away, there was nothing to be seen of the fleeing merchantman. There was only the destroyer visible, making for the scene of the disaster. One and all experienced feelings of exultation and relief. We prayed for happiness in a future existence of the departed warrior and then surfaced in the gathering darkness and continued our northward progress. After several days on this course we came to a point three hundred miles from Okinawa.

The kills achieved by the Kaitens had been reported on each occasion after we had speeded away from the scene of action. Since the Kaiten captain was able to use his periscope while proceeding at thirty knots, a hit was rather an easy matter. Even if sighted at fairly long range, it was impossible for a target whose speed is less then twenty knots to get away. Eventually it should be unnecessary to expend a human life in guiding these craft. Good results could have been achieved with radio control, but it was too late for us to contemplate such developments. We had reached the appalling state of affairs where we had only four big submarines left (seven, if three transports were included), and eight obsolete submarines which carried two Kaitens each.

On the evening of August 15, I-58, her crew elated, was running on the surface looking for targets on passage from the vicinity of Okinawa to the Bungo Channel. I was standing on the bridge scanning the horizon in the direction of the setting sun when I was suddenly called to the hatch by the senior wireless rating. I thought I had never seen a man so sad. He looked ready to burst into tears at any minute. "Please come down a minute," he said. Reluctantly I followed him down, and, drawing me to a corner of the ward room, he said, "Look what's come." It was a communiqué announcing the end of hostilities. I felt stunned, but after considering for a moment I decided it could only be some newspaper stunt, not an official signal. Taking a grip on myself, I said,

"This may be a broadcast for purposes of a *démarche*. Destroy it and throw it away." One of the officers standing nearby who had always been professionally interested in enemy broadcasts remarked, "If it is a *démarche*, it's a very skillful one." I announced to the crew that we could not make a decision to retire on the strength of a press broadcast. In the absence of official orders we would continue to fight. I ordered the wireless rating to bring all telegrams to me in the rough, just as they came, and enjoined him that no one else was to be informed. Thus I decided not to tell the crew about it, for even though it were an official order, no form of carelessness could be permitted while at sea. In a submarine a mistake by any one of the crew in carrying out their duties when diving or surfacing was more to be feared than the enemy. One mistake might easily bring disaster. So I decided to allow them to carry on, in their elated condition, until we got closer to home waters, where we would no longer need to submerge. While having a talk with the surgeon, I was considerably embarrassed when he said, "Aren't we going to hear something rather surprising when we get home?"

We continued diving and surfacing as occasioned by enemy movements and did not for one instant relax our vigilance. Thus we returned to the special craft base on August 17, 1945. I saw a motor boat from shore coming out to us. At last the final moment had come. "Clear lower deck—everybody aft." All the crew assembled aft on the upper deck, which looked rather bare with only the Kaiten chocks remaining. Then, amid tears, I read aloud the Imperial dispatch announcing the end of the war. Without another word I went aboard the motor boat with the messenger and went ashore to report to the senior officer concerning the valiant deeds of our fine Kaiten warriors. They had not survived to suffer the indignity of defeat.

On that day, August 18, 1945, we were met by six HA-class submarines as we passed through the special submarine training area, and together we returned to Kure. Except for one or two dissentients, most of us were past argument, but there were some who were all for going out to fight. Still, it was all over and this minority were confusing their hopes with fact. As we made our weary way homeward, there were some aircraft boisterously dropping pamphlets expressing opposition to the ending of hostilities. We, however, upheld the national constitution and laid down our arms in accordance with the Imperial order.

Let the spirits of the eighty departed warriors of the Kaitens and midgets bear witness! Our country will have to follow a difficult road and the ordeal imposed by heaven on our nation and people continues.

CONCLUSION

By S. Fukutome,
former Chief of Staff,
Combined Fleet,
Imperial Japanese Navy

Failure of Submarines in the Hawaiian Operations:

Prior to the attack on Pearl Harbor by our air units under the command of Vice-Admiral Nagumo, Japanese
submarines were surrounding the island of Oahu and
sitting astride the U. S. lines of communication between
Hawaii and the American mainland. In addition, preparations were complete for sending five midget submarines to penetrate Pearl Harbor.

These submarines, comprising twenty-seven of the latest from the Combined Fleet Submarine Units, and under the command of Vice-Admiral Shimizu, sailed from Kure and Yokosuka between November 18 and 20, 1941.

After taking on fuel and provisions in the Marshalls they proceeded as the advanced guard of Admiral Nagumo's striking force, with the primary object of cutting off ships of the enemy fleet which escaped the consequences of our air strike and, by stopping reinforcements and supplies from the U. S. mainland, so rounding off the whole of the Hawaiian operation. In fact the operations staff in Tokyo expected more from the longer-term submarine warfare than the momentary air strike. However, the results were entirely contrary to expectation and only one out of twenty-seven submarines was able to make any attack. Morison* in his history writes:

> Aggressive patrolling and depth-charging by destroyers and other ships on patrol completely nullified the work of the big 1,900-ton Japanese submarines. They did not torpedo a single one of the very numerous ships entering and departing from Pearl Harbor and Honolulu. Most of the twenty "I" boats deployed south of Oahu returned to Japan within a few days, but about five were ordered to the west coast of the U.S.A. One of these, I-170, was sunk by a plane from the USS *Enterprise*, en route, the others sank a few ships off California and Oregon. Thus the Advanced Expeditionary force failed completely. It inflicted no dam-

---

* Samuel Eliot Morison, *History of United States Naval Operations in World War II* (Little, Brown and Co., Boston, the Atlantic Monthly Press, and O.U.P., London, 1948), Vol. III.

age but lost all five midget submarines and one large one.

Furthermore, when they returned to harbor after the operation, both the senior officers of units and captains of submarines reported as follows:

"The Hawaiian defenses are very sound and the enemy ships in general very much on their guard, making it impossible for submarines to enforce a blockade or cut the lines of communication. Enemy antisubmarine vessels and patrol aircraft kept up a relentless pressure and although our submarines did sight a few targets, they were counterattacked before getting a chance to put in their own attack.

"The submarine is a weapon for attacking merchant ships, i.e., its main function is commerce destruction."

Both Imperial Headquarters and the Combined Fleet were badly shaken by the results of the submarine operations at Hawaii and they were bitterly disappointed with their complete failure. As a result the faith of the Japanese Navy in submarines came to waver.

Submarine Training Based on a War of Attrition:

In the first place Japan failed to secure her desired seventy per cent strength *vis-à-vis* America at the 1922 Washington Naval Treaty, but she calculated to make good this deficiency by means of submarine warfare.

Thus came into being the new tactical method peculiar to Japan—"Attritional Warfare." That is to say, our policy was to use submarines to pick off units of the U. S. fleet as it made its way via Hawaii across the Pacific, and very far-reaching results were expected from such tactics. This policy was strongly advocated by Admiral Suetsugu who held that the success or failure of these tactics would be the turning point in the decisive battle between the two navies and he insisted on relentless training to this end.

In other countries the primary use of submarines was in attacking merchant ships and in commerce destruction, attacks on warships being a secondary object. This policy made the best use of the special features of the submarine and furthermore the loss of valuable cargoes to the enemy was considered of primary importance. Moreover attacks by submarines on closely escorted fleets were of a very hazardous nature. In Japan, however, the reduction of a heavily escorted U. S. warship fleet took precedence over all other targets and intensive training to this end was pursued, and there were frequent and lamentable cases of the sacrifice of submarines on peacetime maneuvers. Despite these occurrences the Japanese Navy went ahead with its plans to pierce the heavily escorted ranks of the enemy, and achieved the necessary confidence to attack warship targets. In fact there was a feeling of almost supernatural skill in the competence with which our submarines carried out their attacks in training and on maneuvers.

Under these circumstances the Japanese Navy expected much from their submarines and at the same time vastly underrated the capabilities of the American submarines. As the submarine campaign at Hawaii showed, our submarine attacks against warships completely misfired and the subsequent attacks on merchant ships achieved little. As opposed to this, our losses at the hands of U. S. submarines were very high and it would not be an overstatement to say that U. S. submarines dealt Japan a mortal blow. The following announcement was made by Ernest J. King, the Chief of U. S. Naval Staff. "U. S. submarines played a very big part in bringing Japan to submission—sixty-three per cent of Japanese ships of over one thousand tons were sunk by submarine, the remaining thirty-seven per cent being accounted for by the other armed forces."

The figures estimated by the Japanese Navy for total shipping losses were 1,000,000 tons in the first year of the war and 800,000 tons in each succeeding year. In actual fact, however, the losses were as follows: First year, 1,250,000 tons; second year, 2,560,000 tons; third year, 3,480,000 tons, i.e., more than four times the estimated amount.

How did the Japanese Navy come to make such an inaccurate estimate? It was because they underestimated the U. S. submarines. Naturally enough the greater proportion of losses was probably expected to be inflicted by submarines, but the greater part of Japan's sea lifelines lay along the routes to the areas of natural resources in the Southern Seas, comprising the Luchu Islands, Formosa, Philippines, Borneo, Celebes, Java, Sumatra, which were defended by a series of natural barricades. We had thought therefore that we could ward off the attacks of enemy submarines by our antisubmarine defenses in the comparatively narrow stretches of sea between these various islands. In the first year of the war alone, losses were heavy in connection with our southern advance and this was probably aggravated by the fact that our antisubmarine measures were undeveloped. But after the second year we might have expected a decrease in losses as our defenses were then in order, but the U. S. submarines proceeded to carry all before them.

Dr. Jerome Bernard Cohen wrote:

> The U. S. blockade of Japan increased in intensity, the supply of raw materials was cut off, and war production was virtually brought to a standstill before the strategic bombing commenced. For this reason Japan was unable to continue the fight. . . .
>
> For every ton she built, Japan was losing three tons by sinking, thus setting at nought her merchant fleet. It was her reliance on the import of raw materials that brought Japan to the brink of misfortune. Matters progressed from bad to worse. The waste in shipping prevented the import of raw materials and steel production was thereby drastically reduced. This reacted on the shipbuilding industry and Japan was unable to make good her shipping losses, and she experienced economic strangulation. At the beginning of 1945 she was at death's door and the air attacks supplied the finishing touches.

What Was the Reason for Such a Pitiable Result?

The losses inflicted by U. S. submarines were not limited to merchant ships. The enemy proceeded to attack our warships with a quite unexpectedly efficient technique. Our losses were stupendous. On June 15, 1944, having heard that the U. S. forces had landed on Saipan, the C.-in-C. Combined Fleet, Admiral Toyoda, collected together all his available forces with the idea of counterattacking in a decisive battle and breaking up the enemy plans. One task force under the command of Vice-Admiral Ozawa began searching for the enemy from dawn on June 18 and by afternoon had sighted three groups of U. S. task forces containing six aircraft carriers to the west of Saipan. As the hour was late and the range excessive, he anticipated an action on the following day. At dawn on the 19th while carrying out a search he sighted an enemy task force in four groups, and at about 8 A.M. and 10 A.M., he launched the first and second attacks respectively. Vice-Admiral Ozawa's flagship, the *Taiho*, was hit by torpedoes from an enemy submarine after launching the first attack and sank with a big explosion six hours later. The aircraft carrier *Shokaku* also was torpedoed by an enemy submarine at about the same time as the flagship. Vice-Admiral Ozawa, despite these losses, determined on a third air attack but there were less than a hundred aircraft remaining and that night he retired westward in expectation of action the next morning. On the afternoon of the following day, the 20th, he was attacked by three hundred enemy planes. The aircraft carrier *Zuikaku* was hit by several bombs and the carrier *Hitaka* was hit by torpedo bombers, and while drifting out of control she was torpedoed and sunk by an enemy submarine. Thus Ozawa's squadron was picked off by submarines while engaged in air combat with the enemy task force. These carriers were strongly escorted by destroyers throughout the action, but the U. S. submarines penetrated our lines without any difficulty and carried out their attacks on large warships.

In October, 1944, Kurita's fleet was intending to penetrate into Leyte Gulf to keep up the attacks on the enemy.

On October 23, while on the lookout at the entrance to the Palawan Channel, the flagship *Atago* and the *Nachi* were sunk by a U. S. submarine, another very serious loss.

Furthermore there were many instances of U. S. submarines picking off even our antisubmarine vessels which were charged with the duty of affording protection from submarines. What were the reasons for these deplorable results? They were largely due to our inferiority in the fields of ordnance and ship construction. Our submarines, built and equipped with inferior weapons, were counterattacked by the enemy before they ever got to their targets, or were evaded. Against the superior equipment of the enemy submarines our ships under attack had no opportunity to counterattack or evade. Many of them were alive to the enemy's presence only after they were attacked.

In the matter of building large-type submarines, Japan was in the lead among the world navies, and had built the two-thousand-ton I class as compared with the biggest in the American and British navies at fifteen hundred tons. Furthermore, during the war, Japan built some thirty-five-hundred-ton submarine aircraft carriers. On six occasions the superior I-class boats of the Japanese Navy were sent to Germany and while at the secret German submarine base of Lorient on the Atlantic coast of France, German submarine technicians made detailed inspections. The Germans criticized the excessive hull vibration and the excessive use of underwater signaling devices, etc., which were not conducive to the tricky conditions of underwater warfare. Submarine

I-39, commanded by Commander Kinashi, was torpedoed and sunk by a U. S. submarine in the Formosa Strait on her return voyage from Germany. This was entirely due to inferior radar equipment. Captain Kinashi is said to have remarked when he put in at Singapore on this last voyage that he had no worry concerning enemy aircraft and submarines as the radar equipment had been greatly improved. On hearing of the many deficiencies in Japanese submarines, Hitler presented two German submarines to Japan to serve as models. One of them, with a German crew, arrived at Kure in July, 1943, but the other one was sunk in the Atlantic by Allied aircraft while en route to Japan with a Japanese crew. These German submarines were of the small seven-hundred-fifty-ton type and were therefore of little value to Japan.

The Japanese Navy expected much from its submarines, and for this reason alone both officers and men were carefully selected and put through the most rigorous training. They considered themselves superior in technique in the field of submarine warfare to any in other navies. But when it came to the test of actual warfare, the results were deplorable. At the end of the war, however, it can be said that slight improvements had been effected in the radar and other electrical equipment fitted in the Japanese Submarine Fleet.

GLOSSARY

GLOSSARY OF
TECHNICAL TERMS
COMPILED BY
THE AUTHOR

ACOUSTIC MINE: A mine which explodes on picking up the
sound waves from a ship's propeller.

ADJUSTING TANK: For adjusting the trim of the boat when
submerged by admitting or discharging sea water.

AIR BOTTLE: Container for storing compressed air.

ANTISUBMARINE NET: A wire net put out by the enemy to prevent entry of submarines. Mines are usually attached to
them.

ASSISTANT TORPEDO OFFICER: Works under the torpedo officer and is responsible for the firing of torpedoes.

ASTRONOMICAL OBSERVATIONS: Observing the height of the sun and stars to ascertain the ship's position.

AUTOMATIC TRIMMING DEVICE: Invented by Constructor-Commander Tomonaga and was in use from the beginning of the war. A device for preserving a constant depth when submerged without moving the propellers. The device is very sensitive to a change in the water pressure and automatically causes the admittance or discharge of water in order to preserve the set depth.

BLOW: The high-pressure air from the air bottles is admitted to the tanks to expel the water therefrom.

CHIEF ELECTRICIAN: In charge of the electrical equipment under the chief engineer.

CHIEF ENGINEER: Responsible for all machinery in the boat.

CONTROL PANEL: Switchboard (electric).

DEEP DIVING DEPTH: Deep depth—usually signifies a depth near to the safety limit.

DEPTH GAUGE: The pressure of water varies with the depth and the gauge is so constructed to record the depth according to the changes in water pressure.

DIRECTION-FINDING EQUIPMENT: Mechanism which records the direction of external radio waves.

DIRECTOR: A calculator used when aiming the guns and torpedoes.

DISCHARGE PUMP: For discharging water from the boat, it is normally used for expelling water from the adjusting tank when submerged. It is also used for getting rid of any water accumulated in the bilges of the boat.

GOING ASTERN: Making the ship go stern-first. Speed is very much slower than going ahead.

GREAT CIRCLE TRACK: The shortest distance between two points on the earth's surface, being the line joining two points on a chart made to Mercator's projection.

GUNNERY OFFICER: In charge of guns and machine guns.

GYRO COMPASS: (GYRO for short) A compass in which a revolving wheel is used instead of a magnet.

HORIZONTAL RUDDER: *See* HYDROPLANE.

HYDROPLANE: For the purpose of keeping the boat at the desired depth when dived. In the latest type of submarines, it can be housed when the boat is on the surface.

KINGSTON VALVES: In the bottom of the main ballast tanks, they admit or release water when diving or surfacing. They are also check valves. It takes about five minutes to operate them and in wartime they are usually left open to facilitate rapid diving.

LOW-PRESSURE AIR DISCHARGE PUMP (LOW-PRESSURE BLOWER): Used for discharging water from the main ballast tanks when surfacing after the conning hatch has been opened and air from outside admitted. This economizes in the use of high-pressure air.

LOW-PRESSURE PIPES: Pipes through which low-pressure air passes. Low-pressure air passes through the low-pressure distributing valves to the individual main ballast tanks.

MAGNETIC MINE: A mechanical mine which explodes due to the induced magnetism of the ship's bottom. It is usually moored on the sea bottom.

MAIN BALLAST TANK: Fitted outboard on both sides of the boat, which can be dived or surfaced by admitting or expelling sea water respectively. It is usual to keep fuel in part of the main tanks.

MAIN BATTERIES: Storage batteries which are charged when proceeding on the surface or using the SCHNORKEL and taking in air, the main engines driving the dynamo. A submarine's motive power when submerged.

NAVIGATOR: Fixes the boat's position and assists the captain with the boat's movements.

NEGATIVE-BUOYANCY TANK (QUICK-DIVING TANK): For making the boat heavier to dive quickly. The water is discharged from them by air when the required depth has been reached.

PERISCOPE: A kind of telescope with which the range of the target can be measured according to the graduations. The size of the object glass is small by day and large by night. Photographs also can be taken through the periscope.

PRESSURE HULL: The outer skin of the submarine designed to withstand the pressure of the sea water. The safe depth to which the boat can dive is calculated from the strength of the pressure hull.

RADAR: Equipment which records the position and range of the target by receiving the reflected waves from electrical impulses transmitted from own ship.

RADAR-SEARCH RECEIVER: Apparatus which takes in enemy transmissions only.

RADIO SHORT-WAVE MAST: Short-wave aerial used in submarines. Can be used for transmission and reception when extended only one meter above the surface.

RANGEFINDER: Distance-finding equipment.

RESIDUARY WATER: Is the water which accumulates inside the boat. It is normally collected in the ship's bilges.

RUDDER: As for a surface vessel.

SAFE DIVING DEPTH: The depth to which the boat may safely dive and at which the pressure hull still withstands the pressure of the water. This depth is calculated from the strength of the pressure hull and allows for a margin of safety. If the boat goes deeper there is a danger that the hull will be crushed.

SHOCK-ABSORBED DEPTH GAUGE (Air-damped): Different from the ordinary depth gauge, it records the depth by measuring the amount of compression due to the water pressure on the air in a glass tube.

STANDARD SPEED: In submarines normally about 12 knots. Each increase by 2 knots is known as Nos. 1, 2, and 3 war speeds respectively. If a submarine has a maximum speed of 16 knots, it cannot, of course, run above No. 2 war speed.

TELEMOTOR OIL-PRESSURE GEAR: The vents and Kingston

valves are usually operated by means of oil pressure on the hydraulic system.

THREE-WATCH CRUISING: The crew is divided into three sections, each of which supplies the necessary watchkeepers when the ship is cruising. Those not on watch are normally completely off duty and asleep or resting.

TORPEDO OFFICER: In submarines is usually the first lieutenant and executive officer. He is directly responsible to the captain for diving and surfacing operations.

TORPEDO TUBES: Tubes for discharging the torpedoes. Number varies according to the class of boat. They are sometimes fitted in the stern as well as in the bow.

TRIMMING PUMP: For transferring water from tank to tank to keep the boat level when submerged.

UNDERWATER SOUND APPARATUS: Mechanism which records underwater sound waves, including the tone and direction of the sounds.

VENTS: Valves for letting out the air from ballast tanks' vent valves.

APPENDIX A

1. Details of Japanese Submarines in Existence at the Outbreak of War

(The details shown in this table apply to a representative ship of each class. There were differences among ships of the same class, and this applied particularly to the I-1, I-53, and I-68 class, where the differences were quite extensive.)

Type of Submarine	Medium			Mine-Laying	Fleet	
Class	RO-57	RO-60	RO-33	I-121	I-68*	I-53*
Ships in the Class	RO-57, 58, 59	RO-60, 61, 62, 63, 64, 65, 66, 67, 68	RO-33, 34	I-121, 122, 123, 124	I-168, 169, 170, 171, 172, 173, 174, 175	I-153, 154, 155, 156, 157, 158, 159, 160, 162, 164,165, 166
Standard Displacement (tons)	(3) 889	(9) 998	(2) 700	(4) 1,142	(8) 1,400	(12) 1,635
Guns	One 8-cm.	One 8-cm.	One 8-cm.	One 15-cm.	One 10-cm.	One 12-cm.
Torpedoes	10†	14†	10†	12†	14†	16
Miscellaneous	—	—	—	Equipped for laying 42 mines	—	—
Surface Speed (knots)	17	16	19	14.5	23	20
Surface Range (nautical miles)‡	Not available	8/5,500	12/800	8/10,500	10/14,000	10/10,000
Safety Depth (feet)	195	195	245	195	245	195
Operational Time Range (days)	20†	20†	30†	20	45†	30†
Crew	40†	43	50†	44	68	89

* From May 20, 1942, the I-53 and I-68 class had 100 added, and became I-153 and I-168. In this book the later numbers have been used from the start. In 1944 two further classes, I-52 and I-54, were built.

† Estimated figures only.

‡ 8/5,500 denotes a range of 5,500 miles at 8 knots; 12/800: 800 miles at 12 knots, etc.

APPENDIX A—continued.

1. DETAILS OF JAPANESE SUBMARINES IN EXISTENCE AT THE OUTBREAK OF WAR—continued.

(The details shown in this table apply to a representative ship of each class. There were differences among ships of the same class, and this applied particularly to the I-1, I-53, and I-68 class, where the differences were quite extensive.)

TYPE OF SUBMARINE	SMALL PATROL			LARGE PATROL	
CLASS - - - - -	I-15	I-16	I-1	I-9	I-7
SHIPS IN THE CLASS - - -	I-15, 17, 19, 21, 23, 25, 26	I-16, 18, 20, 22, 24	I-1, 2, 3, 4, 5, 6	I-9, 10	I-7, 8
	(7)	(5)	(6)	(2)	(2)
STANDARD DISPLACEMENT (tons) -	1,950	2,180	1,955	2,200	1,955
GUNS - - - - -	One 14-cm.	One 14-cm.	Two 12-cm.	One 14-cm.	Two 14-cm.
TORPEDOES - - - -	17	20	17	18	20
MISCELLANEOUS - - -	1 Aircraft	Equipped to carry midget	—	1 Aircraft	1 Aircraft
SURFACE SPEED (knots) - -	24	24	24	18	23
SURFACE RANGE (nautical miles) ‡ -	16/16,000	16/14,000	12/17,500	16/16,400	16/14,000
SAFETY DEPTH (feet) - -	325	325	260	325	325
OPERATIONAL TIME RANGE (days) -	90	90	60	90	60
CREW - - - - -	94	95	68	100	80

‡ 8/5,500 denotes a range of 5,500 miles at 8 knots; 12/800: 800 miles at 12 knots, etc.

APPENDIX A—continued.

2. DETAILS OF JAPANESE SUBMARINE CONSTRUCTION AFTER THE OUTBREAK OF WAR

(The details in this table apply to a representative ship of each class. There were minor differences among ships of the same class.)

TYPE OF SUBMARINE	TRANSPORT			TANKER	AIRCRAFT CARRIERS		SUBMARINES WITH HIGH UNDERWATER SPEED	
CLASS	HA-101	I-371	I-361	I-351	I-13	I-400	HA-201	I-201
SHIPS IN THE CLASS	HA-101, 102, 103, 104, 105, 106, 107, 108, 109, 111 (10)	I-371, 372, 373 (3)	I-361, 362, 363, 364, 365, 366, 367, 368, 369, 370 (10)	I-351 (1)	I-13, 14 (2)	I-400, 401, 402 (3)	HA-201, 202, 203, 204, 205, 207, 208, 209, 210 (9)	I-201, 202, 203 (3)
STANDARD DISPLACEMENT (tons)	370	1,660	1,470	2,650	2,620	3,430	320	1,000
GUNS	—	Four 8-cm.	Four 14-cm.	Two 8-cm.	—	One 14-cm.	—	—
TORPEDOES	—	—	—	4	15	24	4	10
MISCELLANEOUS	—	—	—	—	2 Aircraft	3 Aircraft	—	—
SURFACE SPEED (knots)	10	13	13	16.3	17	18.7	10.5	15.8
SURFACE RANGE (nautical miles)†	10/3,000	13/5,000	10/15,000	14,/12,000	16/21,000	14/37,500 16/30,000	10/3,000	14/5,800
SAFETY DEPTH (feet)	325	325	245	315	325	325	325	355
OPERATIONAL TIME RANGE (days)	15	30	60	60	90	90	15	25
CREW	21	60	45	77	108	144	22	31

† 10/3,000 denotes a range of 3,000 miles at 10 knots; 13/5,000: 5,000 miles at 13 knots, etc.

APPENDIX A—continued.

2. DETAILS OF JAPANESE SUBMARINE CONSTRUCTION AFTER THE OUTBREAK OF WAR—continued.

(The details in this table apply to a representative ship of each class. There were minor differences among ships of the same class.)

TYPE OF SUBMARINE	MEDIUM		FLEET	PATROL		LARGE PATROL	
CLASS	RO-100	RO-35	I-176	I-54	I-15*	I-52	I-9*
SHIPS IN THE CLASS	RO-100, 101, 102, 103, 104, 105, 106, 107, 108, 109, 110, 111, 112, 113, 114, 115, 116, 117 (18)	RO-35, 36, 37, 38, 39, 40, 41, 42, 43, 44, 45, 46, 47, 48, 49, 50, 55, 56 (18)	I-176, 177, 178, 179, 180, 181, 182, 183, 184, 185 (10)	I-54, 56, 58 (3)	I-27, 28, 29, 30, 31, 32, 33, 34, 35, 36, 37, 38, 39, 40, 41, 42, 43, 44, 45 (19)	I-52, 53, 55 (3)	I-11, 12 (2)
STANDARD DISPLACEMENT (tons)	525	965	1,500	1,950	1,950	2,095	2,200
GUNS	—	One 8-cm.	One 12-cm.	One 14-cm.	One 14-cm.	Two 14-cm.	One 14-cm.
TORPEDOES	8	10	12	19	17	19	18
MISCELLANEOUS	—	—	—	1 Aircraft	1 Aircraft	—	1 Aircraft
SURFACE SPEED (knots)	16	19.5	23	18	24	18	24
SURFACE RANGE (nautical miles)†	12/3,500	12/11,000	16/8,000	16/21,000	16/16,000	16/21,000	16/16,400
SAFETY DEPTH (feet)	245	260	260	325	325	325	325
OPERATIONAL TIME RANGE (days)	21	40	75	90	90	90	90
CREW	38	62	86	94	94	94	100

* Estimated figures only.

† 10/3,000 denotes a range of 3,000 miles at 10 knots; 13/5,000: 5,000 miles at 13 knots, etc.

APPENDIX B *(See Chapter 5)*

CLAIMS OF COMMERCE SINKINGS BY JAPANESE SUBMARINES

1. INDIAN OCEAN, 1942–43

SUBMARINE	OPERATIONAL AREA	NUMBER OF SHIPS SUNK	PERIOD
I-159	SW Sumatra	2	Dec., 1941–Jan., 1942
I-162 164	Madras-Cochin	Several*	Early Feb., 1942
I-165 166	SW Sumatra and off Rangoon	Several*	Late Jan., 1942
I-124 123 121 122	North of Australia	1	—
I-4 6 7	South of Christmas Island	1	Late Feb.–early March, 1942
I-1 2 3	West coast of Australia	3	Early March, 1942
I-165 166	Ceylon	4	Feb., 1942
I-159	SW Sumatra	1	Late Feb.–mid-March, 1942
I-162 164	Madras-Cochin	Several*	March, 1942

* It has been impossible to ascertain the exact numbers and types of ships sunk in these areas at these times.

CLAIMS OF COMMERCE SINKINGS BY JAPANESE SUBMARINES
—continued.

SUBMARINE	OPERATIONAL AREA	NUMBER OF SHIPS SUNK	PERIOD
I-7, 4 2, 5 3, 6	Chagos archipelago —Bombay	Approx. 7	—
I-10 16 18 20	Mozambique Channel	12 10	June 5–12, 1942, June 20–mid-July, 1942
I-162 164 165	Indian coast and Bay of Bengal	7	Early Aug.–mid-Nov., 1942
I-29 27	Arabian Sea and east coast of Africa	5	Early Aug.–early Oct., 1942
I-165 166	Arafura Sea	—	Early Dec., 1942
I-29 27	Arabian Sea	1	Mid.-Nov., 1942– March, 1943
I-27	Arabian Sea	4 (inc. a gunboat)	Apr., 1943
I-29 37	Arabian Sea	3	June–Aug., 1943
I-10	Chagos archipelago	1	July–Aug., 1943

APPENDIX B *(See Chapter 5)—continued.*

CLAIMS OF COMMERCE SINKINGS BY JAPANESE SUBMARINES
—continued.

SUBMARINE	OPERATIONAL AREA	NUMBER OF SHIPS SUNK	PERIOD
I-10	Arabian Sea	4	Aug.–Oct., 1943
I-27	Andaman Channel	2	Aug.–Sept., 1943
I-27	Gulf of Aden	2	Oct.–Dec., 1943
I-37	Mozambique Channel	1	Sept.–Dec., 1943
I-162 165 166	Bay of Bengal	1	Sept.–Nov., 1943

Total sinkings: 80 (estimated figure)
Own losses: 2 submarines

2.   BY THE EASTERN AREA ADVANCED FORCE

SUBMARINE	OPERATIONAL AREA	NUMBER OF SHIPS SUNK	PERIOD
I-24	South of Sydney	3	
I-27	Tasmania— New Caledonia	1	Early June, 1942– late July, 1942
I-22	New Zealand— Cook Strait Auckland—Suva	—	
I-19 I-21	Off Brisbane Off Sydney	— —	

APPENDIX B *(See Chapter 5)—continued.*

CLAIMS OF COMMERCE SINKINGS BY JAPANESE SUBMARINES
—continued.

3. BY 3RD SUBMARINE SQUADRON

SUBMARINE	OPERATIONAL AREA	NUMBER OF SHIPS SUNK	PERIOD
I-11	South of Sydney	2	
I-174 175	North of Sydney	2	Late July, 1942– early Aug., 1942
I-169	Vicinity of New Caledonia	1	
I-171	Fiji—Samoa area	—	

4. BY 7TH SUBMARINE SQUADRON

SUBMARINE	OPERATIONAL AREA	NUMBER OF SHIPS SUNK	PERIOD
RO-33	Off Port Moresby	—	Late July–early Aug., 1942
RO-34	Off Santa Isabel Island	1	Late July–early Aug., 1942

Total sinkings (2, 3, and 4): 10 ships
Own losses: none

APPENDIX B *(See Chapter 5)— continued.*

CLAIMS OF COMMERCE SINKINGS BY JAPANESE SUBMARINES
—continued.

5. DURING ATTACKS ON COMMUNICATION LINES AFTER THE WITHDRAWAL FROM GUADALCANAL

SUBMARINE	OPERATIONAL AREA	NUMBER OF SHIPS SUNK	PERIOD
I-10	Noumea Auckland Torres Is.	(Reconnaissance only)	From mid-Jan., 1943
I-21	Sydney	6	Mid-Jan.–early Feb., 1943
I-26	Brisbane	2	Latter-half Apr., 1943
I-17 I-19 I-25	Fiji—Samoa	2	End March–early June, 1943
I-178 I-177 I-180 I-174	East coast of Australia	— 1 2 2	Apr.–June, 1943 Apr., 1943 End Apr.–mid-May, 1943 End May–mid-June, 1943

(Submarine I-168 also was dispatched to this area from home waters, but disappeared between Truk and Rabaul. It was later ascertained that she was sunk by a U. S. destroyer. Submarines I-11, 17, 19, 25, and 26 also operated in the Solomons, Fiji, and New Hebrides areas.)

APPENDIX B *(See Chapter 5)—continued.*

CLAIMS OF COMMERCE SINKINGS BY JAPANESE SUBMARINES
—continued.

SUBMARINE	OPERATIONAL AREA	NUMBER OF SHIPS SUNK	PERIOD
I-19	Espiritu Santo and Fiji islands	—	
I-11	Noumea— New Hebrides	1 Cruiser	July, 1943
I-39 RO-35 I-182 I-20	New Hebrides	—	Early Aug., 1943
I-25	Espiritu Santo	(Reconnaissance only)	—
I-17	Espiritu Santo	1	Mid-Aug., 1943
I-19	Fiji Islands	1	Mid-Aug., 1943
I-39	New Hebrides— Espiritu Santo	1 Cruiser	Early Sept., 1943

(I-17 was sunk by enemy surface vessels and aircraft on Aug. 19, 1943. By mid-Oct., 1943 the following submarines failed to return: I-20, 25, 182, and RO-35.)

I-171 I-39 I-181 I-32 I-21 RO-36	South Pacific	1	Mid-Sept.–early Nov., 1943

Total sinkings: 20
Own losses: 7 submarines

APPENDIX C

DETAILS OF JAPANESE SUBMARINE LOSSES AND A
SUMMARY OF THE JAPANESE SUBMARINE CAMPAIGN

(*Note.*—One of the most difficult problems in keeping war records is
the determination and crediting of the sinkings of an enemy's submarine
force. A few of the sinkings given here are still in dispute as to date,
place, or cause, but this table, compiled from Allied sources, is accepted
as accurate in this country at the time of publication. The Japanese list,
on which the author bases many passages in the text, shows some differences from that of the Allies.)

DETAILS OF JAPANESE SUBMARINE LOSSES AND A

SUB-MARINE	DATE	PLACE	CAUSE OF SINKING
	1941		
I-170	Dec. 10	Off Pearl Harbor	U. S. naval aircraft
RO-66	Dec. 17	North of Wake Island	Collision
RO-60	Dec. 29	Kwajalein, Marshall Islands	Stranded
	1942		
I-160	Jan. 17	Sunda Strait	British destroyer
I-124	Jan. 20	Off Darwin	U. S. destroyer and Australian mine sweepers
I-173	Jan. 27	West of Midway	U. S. submarine
I-23	Jan. 29	North of Hawaii	U. S. destroyers
RO-30	Apr. 26	West of Pearl Harbor	U. S. submarine
I-164	May 17	South of Kyushu	U. S. submarine
I-28	May 17	South of Truk	U. S. submarine
RO-32	July 9	Off Alaska	U.S.C.G. cutter, district craft and R.C.A.F. aircraft
I-123	Aug. 28	East of Savo Island	U. S. mine layer
RO-33	Aug. 29	Southeast of Port Moresby	Australian destroyer
RO-61	Aug. 31	Aleutians	U. S. destroyer and naval aircraft
I-33	Sept. 22	Truk	Accident (was salvaged, recommissioned, and wrecked again, southwest of Shikoku, on June 12, 1944)
RO-65	Sept. 28	Kiska, Aleutians	Accident during attack by U. S. army bombers
I-30	Oct. 13	Off Singapore	British mine

DIX C

SUMMARY OF THE JAPANESE SUBMARINE CAMPAIGN

DATE	ACTIONS INVOLVING SUBMARINES	REMARKS
1941 Dec. 7	Attacks on Hawaii and Malaya	*Phase 1* Japan on the offensive. Allied navies not yet equipped with radar.
1942 Feb. 15 Apr. 5	Fall of Singapore Battle off Ceylon	
May 7	Battle of the Coral Sea	*Phase 2* Japan's air strength gradually reduced.
June 3	Japanese land on Aleutians	
June 4	Battle of Midway	
Aug. 7	U. S. forces land on Guadalcanal	*Phase 3* Japan's offensive brought to a halt. Allied navies begin to use radar and assume the offensive.
Aug. 7	First naval battle of the Solomons	
Aug. 24	Second naval battle of the Solomons	
Oct. 11	Naval battle of Savo Island	
Oct. 26	Naval battle of the South Pacific	

DETAILS OF JAPANESE SUBMARINE LOSSES AND A

SUB-MARINE	DATE	PLACE	CAUSE OF SINKING
I-172	Nov. 10	West of San Cristobal	U. S. mine sweeper
I-3	Dec. 10	Off Guadalcanal	U. S. m.t.b.
I-15	Dec.	Off Savo Island	Bombed by U.S. naval aircraft Dec. 16
I-4	Dec. 20	Southeast of Rabaul	U. S. submarine
I-22	Dec. 25	Off southeast New Guinea	U. S. m.t.b.
	1943		
I-18	Jan. 2	Southwest of Rendova Island	U. S. submarine
I-1	Jan. 29	Off Cape Esperance, Guadalcanal	New Zealand trawlers
RO-102	Feb. 11	South of San Cristobal Island	U. S. destroyer and naval aircraft
RO-34	Apr. 4	South of Santa Isabel Island	U. S. destroyer
RO-103	May 15	East of San Cristobal Island	U. S. destroyer and naval aircraft
RO-107	May 28	West of Espiritu Santo	U. S. submarine chaser
RO-35	June 1	South of Solomons	—
I-9	June 10	Northeast of Attu, Aleutians	U. S. submarine chaser
I-31	June 13	North of Kiska, Aleutians	U. S. destroyer
I-7	June 22	Off Kiska, Aleutians	U. S. destroyer
RO-101	July 1	East of Rendova Island	U. S. destroyer
I-25	July 11	East of Kolombangara	U. S. destroyer
I-24	July 27	Southeast of Admiralty Islands	U. S. submarine
I-17	Aug. 19	Off New Caledonia	New Zealand trawler and U. S. naval aircraft
I-178	Aug. 25	Southeast of San Cristobal Island	U. S. destroyer
I-168	Sept. 3	Northwest of Espiritu Santo	U. S. destroyer

— continued.

SUMMARY OF THE JAPANESE SUBMARINE CAMPAIGN—*contd.*

DATE	ACTIONS INVOLVING SUBMARINES	REMARKS
Nov. 12	Third naval battle of the Solomons	*Phase 4*
Nov. 30	Night action off Lunga	Commencement of transport operations and the southern Solomons interception campaign by Japanese submarine.
1943 Jan. 12	U. S. forces land on Aleutians	
Jan. 29	Battle off Rennell Island	
Feb. 9	Fall of Guadalcanal to Allies	
May 11	U. S. landing on Attu Island	
July 4	First night action of Kula Gulf	
July 12	Second night action of Kula Gulf	
Aug. 6	Naval battle of Vella Gulf	

DETAILS OF JAPANESE SUBMARINE LOSSES AND A

SUB-MARINE	DATE	PLACE	CAUSE OF SINKING
I-182	Sept. 9	Surigao Strait, Philippines	U. S. submarine
I-20	Oct. 1	North of Kolomban-gara	U. S. destroyer
I-34	Nov. 12	Off Penang	British submarine
I-35	Nov. 23	Off Tarawa Island	U. S. destroyers
I-19	Nov. 25	West of Makin Island	U. S. destroyer
I-179	Dec. 16	Northwest of New Britain	U. S. naval aircraft
I-39	Dec. 23	Off Savo Island	U. S. destroyer escort
	1944		
I-181	Jan.	Off New Guinea	—
RO-37	Jan. 22	East of San Cristobal Island	U. S. destroyer
I-171	Jan. 31	West of Buka Island	U. S. destroyers
I-40	Feb.	Marshall Islands area	—
RO-39	Feb. 1	East of Wotje Island	U. S. destroyer
RO-110	Feb. 11	Off Vizagapatam	Indian sloop and Australian mine sweepers
I-27	Feb. 12	Southwest of Maldive Islands	British destroyers
I-21	Feb. 14	Northwest of Jaluit	U. S. destroyer and destroyer escort
I-43	Feb. 15	East of Guam	U. S. submarine
RO-40	Feb. 16	Northwest of Roi	U. S. destroyer and mine sweeper
I-11	Feb. 17	East of Marshall Islands	U. S. destroyer
I-42	Mar. 23	Southwest of Palau Islands	U. S. submarine
I-32	Mar. 24	South of Wotje Island	U. S. destroyer escort and submarine chaser
I-169	Apr. 4	Truk	Accident during attack by U. S. naval aircraft
I-2	Apr. 6	East of Admiralty Islands	U. S. destroyer

— *continued.*

SUMMARY OF THE JAPANESE SUBMARINE CAMPAIGN—*contd.*

DATE	ACTIONS INVOLVING SUBMARINES	REMARKS
Nov. 1	Naval battle off Bougainville Island	
Nov. 20	U. S. forces land on the Gilbert Islands	*Phase 5* Marked increase in Japanese submarine losses.
1944 Feb. 1	U. S. forces land on the Marshall Islands	
Feb. 16	U. S. attack on Truk Island	
Mar. 29	U. S. attacks on Palau Islands	

DETAILS OF JAPANESE SUBMARINE LOSSES AND A

SUB-MARINE	DATE	PLACE	CAUSE OF SINKING
RO-45	Apr. 20	Northwest of Saipan	U. S. submarine
I-180	Apr. 26	Southwest of Kodiak	U. S. destroyer escort
I-183	Apr. 28	Off Bungo Channel	U. S. submarine
I-174	Apr. 29	South of Truk	U. S. naval aircraft and destroyers
RO-501	May 13	Mid-Atlantic	U. S. destroyer
I-176	May 16	North of Solomon Islands	U. S. destroyers
I-16	May 19	Northeast of Solomon Islands	U. S. destroyer escort
RO-106	May 21	North of New Ireland	U. S. destroyer escort
RO-104	May 22	South of Caroline Islands	U. S. destroyer escort
RO-116	May 23	South of Caroline Islands	U. S. destroyer escort
RO-108	May 26	Northeast of Admiralty Islands	U. S. destroyer escort
RO-105	May 29	South of Caroline Islands	U.S. destroyer escorts
RO-111	June 10	East of Roi	U. S. destroyer escort
I-5	June 10	South of Caroline Islands	U. S. destroyer
RO-36	June 13	East of Saipan	U. S. destroyer
RO-44	June 15	East of Eniwetok, Marshall Islands	U. S. destroyer escort
RO-114	June 16	West of Tinian	U. S. destroyers
RO-117	June 17	North of Caroline Islands	U. S. naval aircraft
I-184	June 19	Southeast of Guam	U. S. naval aircraft
I-185	June 22	East of Saipan	U. S. destroyer and mine sweeper
I-52	June 24	Mid-Atlantic	U. S. naval aircraft
I-10	July 4	East of Mariana Islands	U. S. destroyer and destroyer escort
I-6	July 13	West of Tinian	U. S. destroyer escort
I-166	July 17	Off Penang	British submarine
RO-48	July 18	East of Guam	U. S. destroyer escort
I-29	July 26	North of Luzon	U. S. submarine

— continued.

SUMMARY OF THE JAPANESE SUBMARINE CAMPAIGN—*contd.*

DATE	ACTIONS INVOLVING SUBMARINES	REMARKS
May 27	U. S. attack on Biak Island	
June 15	U. S. forces land on Saipan	Japanese submarines first equipped with radar for the battle of Saipan Island.

DETAILS OF JAPANESE SUBMARINE LOSSES AND A

SUB-MARINE	DATE	PLACE	CAUSE OF SINKING
I-55	July 28	North of Caroline Islands	U. S. destroyer escorts
RO-42	Sept. 15	East of Yokosuka	U. S. submarine
I-175	Sept. 25	West of Yap	U. S. destroyer escort
I-364	Oct. 2	North of Angaur	U. S. destroyer escort
I-362	Oct. 24	East of Surigao	U. S. destroyer escort
I-54	Oct. 28	Northeast of Surigao	U. S. destroyers
I-45	Oct. 28	East of Dinegat, Philippines	U. S. destroyer escort
I-37	Nov. 12	East of Yap	U. S. destroyer
I-38	Nov. 13	Northeast Pacific	U. S. frigate and mine sweeper
I-26	Nov. 17	East of Samar	U. S. naval aircraft
I-177	Nov. 19	Northeast of Angaur	U.S. destroyer escorts
RO-100	Nov. 25	Northwest of Vella Navella	U. S. mine
I-46	Nov. 27	West of Leyte Island	U. S. destroyers
I-365	Nov. 28	Southeast of Yoko-suka	U. S. submarine
RO-38	Dec.	Central Pacific	—
	1945		
RO-47	Jan. 13	North of Caroline Islands	U. S. destroyer escort
I-48	Jan. 22	Off Ulithi, Western Carolines	U.S. destroyer escorts
RO-115	Jan. 31	Southwest of Manila	U. S. destroyers and destroyer escorts
RO-55	Feb. 7	West of Luzon	U. S. destroyer escort
I-41	Feb. 9	North of Luzon	U. S. submarine
RO-112	Feb. 11	North of Luzon	U. S. submarine
RO-113	Feb. 12	North of Luzon	U. S. submarine
RO-43	Feb. 14	West of Iwo Jima	U. S. naval aircraft
RO-49	Feb. 24	Off Bungo Channel	U. S. submarine
I-370	Feb. 25	South of Iwo Jima	U. S. destroyer escort
I-368	Feb. 26	West of Iwo Jima	U. S. naval aircraft
I-371	Mar. 22	Southeast of Okinawa	U. S. destroyer

—continued.

SUMMARY OF THE JAPANESE SUBMARINE CAMPAIGN—*contd.*

DATE	ACTIONS INVOLVING SUBMARINES	REMARKS
Sept. 15	U. S. forces land on Morotai and Peleliu Islands	
Oct. 20	U. S. Landing on Leyte Island	
1945 Jan. 9	U. S. forces land on Luzon Island	*Phase 6* Unmistakable signs of defeat for Japan. More Japanese submarines equipped with radar. Appearance of human torpedoes.
Feb. 19	U. S. forces land on Iwo Jima	

DETAILS OF JAPANESE SUBMARINE LOSSES AND A

SUB-MARINE	DATE	PLACE	CAUSE OF SINKING
I-8	Mar. 30	Southeast of Okinawa	U. S. destroyers
RO-41	Apr. 4	West of Okinawa	U. S. destroyer
RO-64	Apr. 4	Inland Sea	U. S. mine
RO-67	Apr. 4	North of Shikoku	U. S. mine
RO-46	Apr. 8	East of Okinawa	U. S. destroyers
I-44	Apr. 10	Southeast of Okinawa	U. S. destroyer
I-56	Apr. 17	East of Okinawa	U. S. naval aircraft and destroyers
RO-56	Apr. 17	East of Wake Island	U. S. submarine
RO-109	Apr. 29	Southeast of Okinawa	U. S. naval aircraft
I-12	May 30	Southeast of Okinawa	U. S. naval aircraft
I-361	June	Japanese waters	—
I-122	June 10	Off west coast of Japan	U. S. submarine
I-165	June 27	East of Saipan	U. S. naval aircraft
I-13	July 5	Off east coast of Honshu	U. S. naval aircraft and destroyer escort
I-351	July 14	North of Sarawak	U. S. submarine
I-372	July 28	South coast of Shikoku	U. S. carrier aircraft
I-373	Aug. 13	East China Sea	U. S. submarine

Total losses (excluding midget submarines) : 130 submarines.

— *continued.*

SUMMARY OF THE JAPANESE SUBMARINE CAMPAIGN—*contd.*

DATE	ACTIONS INVOLVING SUBMARINES	REMARKS
Apr. 1	U. S. forces land on Okinawa	
Aug. 16	—	Japanese Emperor orders "Cease Fire."

INDEX

Footnote to the Sinking of the *Indianapolis*

"Shortly after delivering critical parts for the first atomic bomb to be used on Hiroshima to the United States air base at Tinian, the Indianapolis was torpedoed by the Imperial Japanese Navy submarine I-58, sinking in 12 minutes."– *Wikipedia.*

Captain McVay of the *Indianapolis* survived the sinking of his ship, but was court-martialed for negligence soon after. In April 1999 Congress passed a joint resolution exonerating him, and calling on the President to honor him with a posthumous citation:

"Whereas shortly after midnight on the night of July 30, 1945, during the closing days of World War II, the United States Navy heavy cruiser U.S.S. INDIANAPOLIS (CA-35) was torpedoed and sunk by a Japanese submarine;

"Whereas of the 1,196 crew members, only 316 survived the attack and subsequent five-day ordeal adrift at sea, the rest dying from battle wounds, drowning, shark attacks, exposure, or lack of food and water, making the sinking of the INDIANAPOLIS the worst sea disaster in United States naval history…

"Whereas United States military intelligence activities, through a code-breaking system called ULTRA, had learned that the Japanese submarine I-58 was operating in the Philippine Sea area, but Captain McVay was not told of this intelligence, which remained classified as Top Secret until the early 1990's…

"Whereas the commander of that submarine, Mochitsura Hashimoto, testified at the court-martial that once he had detected the ship, he would have been able to make a successful torpedo attack whether or not the ship was zigzagging;

"Whereas Captain McVay thus became the first United States Navy commanding officer brought to trial for losing his ship in combat during World War II, despite the fact that over 700 ships were lost during World War II…

"Captain McVay's conviction was a miscarriage of justice."

McVay did not live to hear the news. Thirty years earlier, in 1968, the burden of blame had led him to shoot himself with his own Navy revolver.

Publisher's Note

A Pacific Polemic

What induced Japan to enter on a suicidal mission of war on the United States? Many have claimed that President Roosevelt had foreknowledge of the attack on Pearl Harbor, and that he even strove to provoke it, in order to bring the US into the war in Europe. But what lay behind the rise of Japanese militarism? Japan had been staunchly isolationist for centuries. How did she come to make war on Russia in 1905, only a few decades after her opening to the West, and then invade China in the 1930's?

One clue is fairly evident: the Japanese war with Russia was financed by the New York banking house of Jos. Schiff & Co., who also put up the money for the 1905 revolution against the Tsar. Schiff was a New York agent of the House of Rothschild, which had grown rich and powerful by lending to both sides in Europe's wars.

"From the founding of the United States, the federal government has relied on subterfuge, skullduggery, and secret operations to advance American interests." – The Hoover Institution.

The first time I wrote a publisher's afterword was in 2002, for *The War on Freedom*. This was the first book in English to suggest that 9/11 was a false-flag covert operation, carried out by the skunk works of the US, against US. The title I gave my polemic then was "Where Would We Be Without Our Wars." Nowadays, especially since the second war on Iraq, I prefer not to pronounce the words "We" and "Our" to identify these horrors. It is They…

The thesis of "WWWBWOW" was that no country – other than Britain – has ever wanted war with the United States! Yet the Anglo-American establishment needs to throw America's military weight around, in order to extend its world domination. The only way to war is to invent excuses and provocations, as in 1846 against Mexico, 1898 against Spain, 1950 against North Korea, 1964 in the Tonkin Gulf, and 1990, the first war on Iraq.

There was a broken link in my argument, though. In 1941 Japan really had attacked the US. That was suicidal folly, of course, as you can only realize even more clearly after reading *Sunk!*

What ever possessed them, and where is the author who will write the book to tell us?

The closest I came to finding one was the late Ohta Ryu. In 2007, two years before his untimely death, he reviewed an article on how the British gained control over 19th-century Japan from the inside, through agents sent by "the Rothschild's man in Asia, Jardine Matheson."

In his short critique, Ryu wrote this tantalizing hint:

"Who could be the agent to implement with success, such an agenda?

"None other than the Showa Emperor.

"The whole Imperial household with Showa Emperor as the Head.

"The thread of entanglement must unravel back to Komei Emperor's assassination to comprehend the current situation of Japan and decipher it with any coherent logic."

The Emperor Komei ruled from 1846 to 1867. He vehemently strove to fend off the unequal treaties and other incursions of the West. According to Wikipedia, "he opposed opening Japan to Western powers, even as the shogun continued to accept foreign demands... Emperor Komei began to assert himself and regain many of the powers his ancestors had conceded to the Tokugawa clan" (the shoguns).

Unluckily for Japan, in 1867 Komei died suddenly of smallpox, though he had always been robustly healthy. The hint is that he was poisoned, and his place usurped by another dynasty subservient to the Anglo-American bankers and their empire. One that would quickly get deep into debt to them for a start... and attack their eternal rival Russia in 1905.

Now in 1941, what the Anglo money power needed was a pretext for a reluctant USA to make war on Germany, so as to cement their rule over Europe. The Japanese emperor – the bankers' man in Japan – provided it on cue at Pearl Harbor.

So is the paradox of the *kamikaze*. In *Sunk!* we read the tragedy of a desperate band of brave souls, like so many from all nationalities, who struggled and died by the millions in the second Great War for no other purpose, than to erect the world dominion of the loan sharks of London and New York.

Divide et impera. When will it be shown and widely known that Japanese militarism, too, was an artificial creation, from the same intriguers who finance both sides of every war for profit, and play divide-and-conquer for world power?

– John-Paul Leonard, publisher,
Progressive Press,
May 2010

http://progressivepress.com
info@progressivepress.com
Tel. 760-366-3695, Fax 366-2937
PO Box 126, Joshua Tree, Calif. 92252.

PROGRESSIVE PRESS PAPERBACKS

Coming Soon for 2010

Dope Inc.: Britain's Opium War against the United States. "The Book that Drove Kissinger Crazy." New edition of the Underground Classic.

Final Warning: A History of the New World Order, by David Allen Rivera. In-depth research nails down the Great Conspiracy in its various aspects as the Fed, the CFR, Trilateral Commission, Illuminati.

Terrorism and the Illuminati, A 3000-Year History, by David Livingstone. "Islamic" terrorists are tentacles of the Illuminati; history of the Luciferian bloodline. 2nd edition.

Understanding The Economic Crisis... 4 Dummies, by Larry Green. Making Sense of the Financial Mess.

Out of Pocket – Rotten Deals, by Bradley Ayers. Caribbean thriller tells the inside story of the CIA's phony war on drugs.

Homeland, by James Hufferd. It's 2032, and our puppet president has agreed to sell the United States to The Company outright...

Global Predator: US Wars for Empire, by Stewart Halsey Ross. A damning account of the "American century" of atrocities by US armed forces.

Trilateral Essays, by Webster Tarpley. Investigative journalism piercing the mask of foul intrigues in foreign and domestic policy, since the regime rotation.

Conspiracy, NWO

Corporatism: the Secret Government of the New World Order, by Prof. Jeffrey Grupp. Corporations control all basic resources of the world, all the governments and institutions, and prevent us from solving humanity's problems. Their New World Order plan is the global "prison planet" Hitler aimed for. 408 pp., $16.95.

The Telescreen: An Empirical Study of the Destruction of Consciousness, by Prof. Jeff Grupp. How the media brainwash us with consumerism, war propaganda, false history, fake news, fake issues, and fake reality. 199 pp., $14.95.

Seeds of Destruction: The Hidden Agenda of Genetic Manipulation, by F. Wm. Engdahl, author of *A Century of War*. A corporate gang is out for complete control of the world by patenting our food. He takes us inside the corporate boardrooms and science labs to reveal a world of greed, intrigue, corruption and coercion. Reads as the crime story it is. 340 pp., $24.95.

The Illuminati. Canadian philosopher Henry Makow, PhD. tackles taboos like Zionism, British Imperialism, and Holocaust denial, as he relates how international bankers stole a monopoly on government credit, and took over the world. They run it all: wars, schools, media. 249 pp., $19.95. Also by Henry Makow, new sequel: *Illuminati 2 - Deceit and Seduction.* Secularism and Satanism. 288 pp., $21.95.

Cruel Hoax: Feminism and the New World Order. The Attack on Your Human Identity. Henry Makow's unusual insights on social and sexual aspects of the conspiracy to enslave humanity. 232 pp., $19.95.

How the World Really Works, by A.B. Jones. A crash course in the conspiracy field. Digests of 11 works like *A Century of War, Tragedy and Hope, Creature from Jekyll Island, Dope Inc.* 336 pp., $15.00.

The Triumph of Consciousness: Overcoming False Environmentalism, Lapdog Media, Global Government, by Chris Clark. The real Global Warming agenda: more hegemony by the NWO. 347 pages, $19.95.

The Complete Patriot's Guide to Oligarchical Collectivism: its Theory and Practice, by Ethan. A nonfictional exploration of Orwell's *1984* for our times, and a guide to taking ownership of our lives and our world. 484 pp., $19.95.

Modern History

The Nazi Hydra in America: Suppressed History of a Century, by Glen Yeadon. Exposes how US plutocrats launched Hitler, then recouped Nazi assets to lay the postwar foundations of a modern police state. Fascists won WWII because they ran both sides. *"The story is shocking and sobering and deserves to be widely read."* – Howard Zinn. 700 pp., $19.95.

Witness in Palestine: A Jewish American Woman in the Occupied Territories, by Anna Baltzer. The nuts and bolts of everyday oppression. Packed with color photos. 400 pp., $26.95.

Enemies by Design: Inventing the War on Terrorism. A century of Anglo-American skullduggery grabbing Gulf oil, in 4 parts: biography of Osama bin Laden; Zionization of America; Afghanistan, Palestine, Iraq; One Nation Under PNAC. An impassioned, relentlessly documented plea. 416 pp., $17.95.

1,000 Americans Who Rule the USA (1947, 324 pp., $18.95) and *Facts and Fascism* (1943, 292 pp., $15.95), by the great muckraking journalist George Seldes – whistleblower on the plutocrats who keep our media in lockstep, and finance fascism. Nothing changed in 65 years: must reading to understand the USA today.

Inside the Gestapo: Hitler's Shadow over the World (1940), by Hansjürgen Koehler. Intimate, fascinating defector's tale of ruthlessness, spy intrigue, geopolitics and bizarre Third Reich personalities. 287 pp., $24.95.

Propaganda for War: How the US was Conditioned to Fight the Great War, by Stewart H. Ross. How propaganda by Britain and her agents like Teddy Roosevelt tricked the USA into the war to smash the old world order. 356 pages, $18.95.

Sunk: The Story of the Japanese Submarine Fleet, 1941-1945. The bravery of doomed men in a lost cause against impossible odds. The kaitens were not the only submarine kamikazes: the whole war was suicide from the start. By Mochitsura Hashimoto, who sank the ship that carried the A-bomb to Tinian. 285 pp., $15.95.

Conspiracy: 9/11 False Flag

9/11 Synthetic Terror: Made in USA. Webster Griffin Tarpley's working model of the 9/11 plot: a rogue network of moles, patsies, and professional killer cells, operating in privatized paramilitary settings, and covered by corrupt politicians and corporate media. The authoritative account of 9/11 as inside job. "Strongest of the 770+ books I have reviewed here at Amazon… most important modern reference on state-sponsored terrorism."– Robert Steele, ex-intelligence officer, #1 non-fiction reviewer on Amazon. 4th edition, 512 pp., $17.95.
In Spanish: ***11-S Falso Terrorismo.*** 408 pp., $19.95.

9/11 on Trial: The W T C Collapse. Presents 20 proofs from math and science that the WTC went down by a controlled demolition. "An enormous amount of important information… very readable." – David Ray Griffin. 192 pp., $12.95.

America's "War on Terrorism" – Concise, wide-reaching, hard-hitting study on 9/11 in geopolitical context, by Prof. Michel Chossudovsky. 387 pp., $22.95.

Conspiracies, Conspiracy Theories and the Secrets of 9/11, from Germany's Top Ten best-seller list. Mathias Broeckers plunges into a fascinating exploration of conspiracy in history, then tackles 9/11. 274 pages, $14.95.

The War on Freedom. The classic exposé of evidence of malfeasance by a neo-con clique that led to the events of 9/11/2001. "Far and away the best and most balanced analysis of September 11th." – Gore Vidal. 400 pp., $16.95.

Truth Jihad: My Epic Struggle against the 9/11 Big Lie. The first humorous book on 9/11, and outrageously so. Barrett sends critics like Sean Hannity, the Secret Service and neocon politicians packing. Insights on academic freedom, bigotry, and media blindness. 224 pp., $12.95.

Terror on the Tube: Behind the Veil of 7/7, an Investigation, by Nicholas Kollerstrom. Only book with the glaring evidence that the four Muslim scapegoats were completely innocent. 7/7 is Bliar's Big Lie and Reichstag Fire, pretext for war and an Orwellian, neo-fascist police state in the UK – and US! 292 pp., $17.77.

9/11 Fiction: ***Skulk! a Post-9/11 Comic Novel,*** by Marc Estrin. A racy parody of political surreality with a stunning ending, this is an engaging truth tool for every activist toolbox. 180 pp., $14.95.

Economics, Financier Oligarchy

Surviving the Cataclysm, ***Your Guide through the Greatest Financial Crisis in Human History***, by Webster G. Tarpley. Richly detailed history of the financier oligarchy, how they plunder our nation. Plus: How to cope with the crisis. 668 pp., $29.95. New revised edition coming in Fall 2010, approx. $19.95.

The Globalization of Poverty and the New World Order, by Prof. Chossudovsky. Brilliant analysis of how corporatism feeds on human poverty, destruction of the environment, apartheid, racism, sexism, and ethnic strife. 401 pp., $24.95.

The Global Economic Crisis: The Great Depression of the XXI Century. Its complex causes, devastating consequences and the corrupt links between the Fed and Wall Street, explained by 16 expert authors. 416 pp., $24.95.

Psychology: Brainwashing

The Rape of the Mind: The Psychology of Thought Control, Menticide and Brainwashing (1956), by Joost Meerloo, M.D. The good Dutch doctor escaped from a Nazi death camp – to discover America's subtler mass mind control. Wide-ranging study of conditioning in open and closed societies, with tools for self-defense against torture or social pressure. 320 pages, $16.95.

Biography, New World Oligarchy

George Bush: The Unauthorized Biography, Tarpley and Chaitkin's vivid X-ray of the oligarchy dominating U.S. politics. Who made fortunes building up Hitler's war machine? Find Bush Sr. linked to Iran-Contra, Watergate, and war crimes. "By far the best exposé of powerful families and their networks...boggles the mind... Absolutely a must-read." 700 pp., $19.95.

Obama – The Postmodern Coup: Making of a Manchurian Candidate. Tarpley reveals that the Obama puppet's advisors are even more radical reactionaries than the neo-cons. A crash course in political science, it distills decades of political insight and astute analysis. 320 pages, $15.95.

Barack H. Obama: the Unauthorized Biography. Webster G. Tarpley at his best: insightful, witty, activist, iconoclastic. This complete profile of a puppet's progress details Obama's doings in the trough of graft and corruption of the Chicago Combine. His regime will be one of economic sacrifice to finance Wall Street bailouts, and for imperialist confrontation with Russia and China. 595 pp., $19.95.

Clown Prince Bush the W. A thoroughly tipsy biography of the late resident anti-hero of the White House, by reporter Ted Cohen. 192 pp., $13.95.

DVDs

By BBC director Adam Curtis:

1) Power of Nightmares, how governments sell terror. All 3 parts, 3 hours. $7.50 in clamshell case. In Amaray case, $11.99.

2) The Century of Self, expose of mass-market brainwashing techniques, and much more. Four hours on one disc, clamshell case, $7.95. Best quality, on two discs, in Amaray box case, $17.95.

3) The Trap. Highly intelligent film exposes the dire effects of materialist behaviorist ideas on society, health, education. Look it up on Wikipedia. 3 hours. Clamshell case, $7.50, Amaray box case, $11.99.

Adam Curtis Trilogy: All 3 programs above, on 4 discs, in Amaray box case, $24. Or, all 3 Adam Curtis single DVDs, clamshell cases: only $20.

4) The Living Dead. 3 hours. Curtis explores how history is manipulated to control us in the present. Clamshell case, $7.95.

ProgRESSive

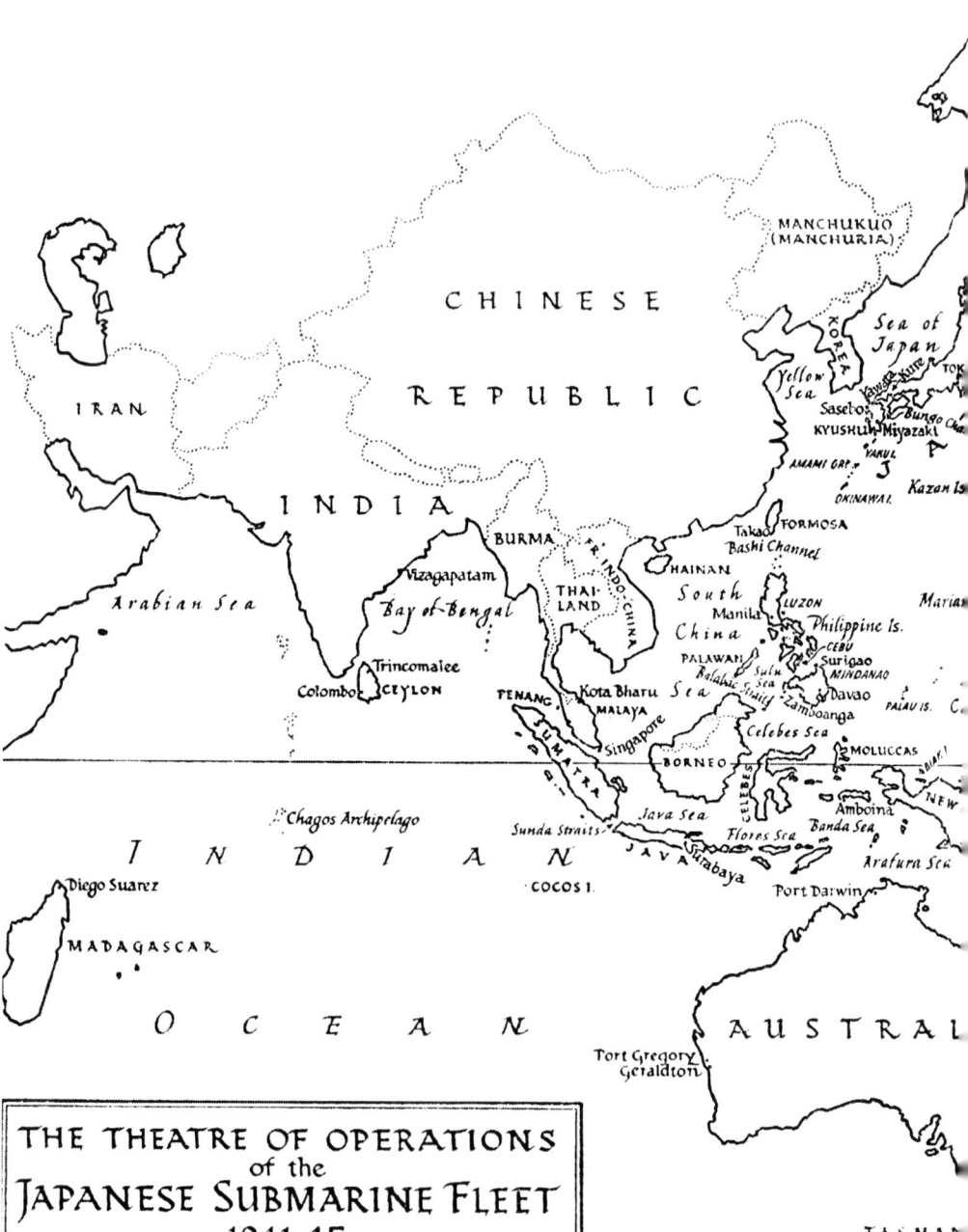

UNION OF SOVIET SOCIALIST REPUB

MANCHUKUO
(MANCHURIA)

CHINESE

REPUBLIC

IRAN

INDIA

Arabian Sea

BURMA

Vizagapatam

Bay of Bengal

THAI-
LAND

FR. INDO-CHINA

HAINAN

South

China

Sea

Trincomalee

Colombo CEYLON

PENANG

Kota Bharu

MALAYA

Singapore

SUMATRA

Chagos Archipelago

Sunda Straits

COCOS I.

Java Sea

JAVA Surabaya

Flores Sea

Diego Suarez

MADAGASCAR

Banda Sea

Arafura Sea

O   C   E   A   N

I   N   D   I   A   N

Port Darwin

Fort Gregory
Geraldton

AUSTRAL

KOREA

*Sea of
Japan*

*Yellow
Sea*

Saseto

KYUSHU Miyazaki

Bungo Cha.

YAKU I.

AMAMI OSH.

OKINAWA I.

Kazan Is.

FORMOSA

Takao

Bashi Channel

Manila LUZON

Philippine Is.

CEBU

PALAWAN

Balabac Strait

Sulu
Sea

MINDANAO

Surigao

Davao

Zamboanga

Celebes Sea

BORNEO

CELEBES

MOLUCCAS

Amboina

PALAU IS.

TOK

Marian

TASMAN

THE THEATRE OF OPERATIONS
of the
JAPANESE SUBMARINE FLEET
1941-45

CPSIA information can be obtained at www.ICGtesting.com
Printed in the USA
BVOW011419130812

297759BV00001B/94/P